A WORLD REMAKING; OR, PEACE FINANCE

Published @ 2017 Trieste Publishing Pty Ltd

ISBN 9780649736973

A World Remaking; Or, Peace Finance by Clarence W. Barron

Except for use in any review, the reproduction or utilisation of this work in whole or in part in any form by any electronic, mechanical or other means, now known or hereafter invented, including xerography, photocopying and recording, or in any information storage or retrieval system, is forbidden without the permission of the publisher, Trieste Publishing Pty Ltd, PO Box 1576 Collingwood, Victoria 3066 Australia.

All rights reserved.

Edited by Trieste Publishing Pty Ltd.
Cover @ 2017

This book is sold subject to the condition that it shall not, by way of trade or otherwise, be lent, re-sold, hired out, or otherwise circulated without the publisher's prior consent in any form or binding or cover other than that in which it is published and without a similar condition including this condition being imposed on the subsequent purchaser.

www.triestepublishing.com

CLARENCE W. BARRON

A WORLD REMAKING; OR, PEACE FINANCE

CLARENCE W. BARRON

A WORLD REMAKING; OR, PEACE FINANCE

Trieste

A WORLD REMAKING

OR

PEACE FINANCE

By
CLARENCE W. BARRON
Author of
"WAR FINANCE" "THE MEXICAN PROBLEM"
"THE AUDACIOUS WAR" ETC.

HARPER & BROTHERS PUBLISHERS
NEW YORK AND LONDON

I DEDICATE THIS BOOK TO MY YOUNGEST GRANDCHILD

MARTHA ENDICOTT

IT IS THE ONLY COMPENSATION I CAN MAKE TO HER FOR GRANDPA'S LONG ABSENCES FROM HOME, AND IS WITH THE HOPE THAT SHE MAY LONG CONTINUE THE EARTHLY LINK IN THE STILL INSPIRING INFLUENCES OF HER MOTHER AND HER GRANDMOTHER, MY FORMER TRAVELING COMPANIONS IN EUROPE.

CONTENTS

CHAP		PAGE
	FOREWORD	ix
I.	ENGLAND THE GREAT WAR LOSER	1
II.	WHAT THE PEOPLE OF ENGLAND DO NOT YET KNOW	8
III.	ENGLAND'S WEAKNESS AND RESTRICTED OUTPUT	19
IV.	COSTS FOR STEEL AND THOUGHT	32
V.	SHIPS AND SHIPPING	45
VI.	ENGLISH SHIPPING AND RAILROADS	56
VII.	THE VALUE OF THE POUND STERLING	64
VIII.	ENGLAND'S PROTECTION POLICY	70
IX.	PROTECTION AND PROTECTED SHIPPING	77
X.	REMAKING ENGLAND IN MEN AND MACHINERY	89
XI.	REDUCING HOURS AND INCREASING EFFICIENCY	99
XII.	THE SPIRIT UNDER BRITISH FINANCE AND BUSINESS	110
XIII.	YANKEE ENTERPRISE IN BRITAIN	119
XIV.	CROWDED PARIS AND OVERCROWDED EUROPE	130
XV.	THE SOCIAL UNREST	135
XVI.	PEACE "WITHOUT VICTORY"	141
XVII.	NOT WRITING BUT MAKING A PEACE	146
XVIII.	HELPLESS RUSSIA	152
XIX.	WORK, NOT FINANCE, THE SITUATION	157
XX.	INDEMNITIES AND SIGNATURES	163

CONTENTS

CHAP.		PAGE
XXI.	SOCIALISM VERSUS DEMOCRACY	171
XXII.	WAR'S INVENTIONS FOR SHIPS	179
XXIII.	INFLATED AND INTERNATIONAL TRADE	185
XXIV.	INFLATION BY CURRENCY, WAR BONDS, AND TAXES	192
XXV.	ARE WE TO PAY FOR GERMAN INTRIGUE AT PANAMA?	202
XXVI.	FOUNDATIONS IN INTERNATIONAL SOCIALISM	211
XXVII.	BOLSHEVIK DANGER AND THE REMEDY	226
XXVIII.	THE PRINCIPLES UNDER WAGES AND PROFITS	236

FOREWORD.

It has been my ambition and life work to find the root causes for economic changes.

Poultney Bigelow well says in his late work on "Prussianism and Pacifism":

"There is no moment in the life of a nation more important than any other. Wars and famines, earthquakes and pestilences—these make convenient aids to memory and help to fasten the attention of uncritical readers. But if history is to serve humanity, its duty is to lay bare the causes of disaster and thus help the legislator to frame better laws for the future."

All history is bound up in the human problems of personal and national finance—personal and national protection to daily subsistence. I visited Europe in the first six months of the war to find its causes, and published my observations in "The Audacious War."

I went to Europe again in the summer and fall of 1918, viewed the scarred battlefields and the devastated cities, traveled the high-

FOREWORD

ways with the forces moving forward and the German prisoners traveling back, and stood under the roar of the guns and the protection of the balloon observers and airplane men. Then I passed around the end of the line into Switzerland and from "the roof of the world" took survey of the negotiations for peace which were begun in January, 1918. I saw the crumbling of the German military Frankenstein monster and hastened home before the armistice to describe the situation and the coming end of the military operations in my articles and book entitled "War Finance."

I visited Europe again in the winter and spring of 1919 to find out what Germany would have to pay in reparation, indemnity and disarmament under the terms of peace.

I found the economists agreed with my first figures that Germany could pay between thirty and forty billion dollars and still have machinery and incentive to recover her industrial position in the world. I found also the undercurrents, the diplomacy and the compromises that forced the real issue of German settlement into the background and brought forward a peace pact of three sections that would first set up a league of nations, or superstate, that would maintain the peace of the world

FOREWORD

by boycotts and edicts of starvation—the denial of food and commerce to disobedient nations—without right of appeal to anybody or court of justice representing the international law which has been building up during the past hundred years.

In the second section it would set up new boundaries for all the people on and beyond the Rhine (including several new republics) and various international mandates and no "self-determinations of peoples."

Thirdly it would give recognition and promise of co-operation with certain indefinite international labor organizations in apparent or veiled recognition of the theories of international socialism and government by international labor organizations as proposed by Heinrich Karl Marx, the author of modern international socialism.

I found the grossest and most cowardly injustice in furtherance of this socialistic program in the abandonment of the people of Russia who had given to the Allies in their war for civilization's defense the greatest human sacrifice.

I found Russia was to be abandoned to the spoliation and exploitation by the men Ger-

FOREWORD

many had sent in during the war for the ruin of the country, the destruction of its powers of self-defense, and the effacement of Russian "self-determination."

I found the same hand that had given our neighbor to the south of us over to internal destruction by brigandage, carrying out the same policy as respects the rest of the world: "Lock 'em in and let 'em fight; but outside we are preserving the peace of the world."

Still let us hope that we have made progress in international peace because we have been forced to think internationally. But we can have sound international agreements only between sound nations with sound principles.

Democracy has made great material success in the United States. Other nations want that material success. They will adopt our principles if we share our prosperity. Our net national debt is 6% of our national wealth. England and France will emerge from the war mortgaged for 50% of their pre-war wealth. Germany should be mortgaged to the allies for as near 50% of her eighty billions of wealth as can be considered collectible without impairment of security.

Viewed from one standpoint, the world outside the United States is in financial and social

FOREWORD

chaos. But it must be remembered that the national debts of France and of England are within their own borders. Whatever may be the talk of Germany reorganizing, drilling and preparing for the next war, little attention need be paid to it. She cannot fight again until she conquers or absorbs Russia or Rumania and gets from one of these countries a vast supply of oil. But the Russian oil fields are declining, and the oil fields of Rumania are within a small area. The British government and the United States will hold the oil fields of the world if Doheny is backed by the United States in possessions which the flag of his nation should insure him, and he is not forced to sell out to Great Britain or some other nation. The Allies "floated to victory on a sea of oil," and not for many generations can Germany again gather up oil, copper or cotton with which to make war on the rest of mankind.

The hope of the world and its civilization now rests upon these United States. To educate her native and foreign-born elements as to the United States Constitution, its meaning and representative government and its true democracy, as contrasted with mobocracy, is the plain duty of the hour.

FOREWORD

From the United States and its true democratic justice must arise the principles which shall scatter the mists of Marxian and German international socialism—poisoner of democracy, enemy of man and of his individual development.

It is in the hope that the facts, the finance, the principles of human fellowship—the true relations between the work of capital and the work of hand, and the relation of both to the labor of brain—as here set forth, may be helpful in the solution of the world problems now before my country, that I submit these articles.

Nowhere in finance or sociology can there be a finality, but that the record may appear in its true or helpful light, the articles are presented with the date of their compilation.

CLARENCE W. BARRON.

A WORLD REMAKING

OR

PEACE FINANCE

I

ENGLAND THE GREAT WAR LOSER

ENGLAND, March, 1919.

OF all the Allies England is the greatest sufferer by the war; yet the world does not know it. Economically, she has been shot to pieces and she does not yet know it.

Ninety-three per cent. of the people of Russia never had anything, and all the sufferers in Russia by the war may number less than the people who have yet to suffer in England. The stings of pride, the hurt to the mind, the loss of place, position and power, may bring pains as sharp as those of physical suffering.

Bolshevism is dying in Russia of exhaustion and Russia has a great new day still ahead in the dawning. When she emerges, all

A WORLD REMAKING

the inventions of the world for production, for communication, and for transportation will be at her service for fruition from the work of 180,000,000 people on the greatest undeveloped soil in the world.

France can live 70 per cent. upon her soil and 30 per cent. by her position in art and world entertainment. She has suffered a great scar in Picardy, but will bound over it and possess potash, iron and coal in provinces on the Rhine beyond her pre-war dreams.

France is self-containant.

Great Britain is an island with exotic industries, dependent upon imports for raw material, with balancing exports of coal and manufactured goods and is buttressed by shipping, colonies and coaling stations around the world.

Economically, financially and industrially she has been sunk. As soon as she finds it out, the question will be how long it will take her, with her noblest sons returned from the wars, to raise anew her industrial banners and again ride the seas in far-flung lines, returning world wealth to her island shores.

When I arrived in England this year on my third war trip, I looked first for the foundations and guarantees of peace. Parchments

ENGLAND THE GREAT WAR LOSER

and preachings are of no avail as compared with practices, and practices are forced by conditions—conditions of food, conditions of shelter, and both are allied to climate and transportation.

Civilization is largely a matter of climate, and the close students of the march of civilization will tell you that England has been developed not from her soil, but from her atmosphere, permitting, and in part forcing, all-the-year-round out-of-door work and exercise.

It is just the climate for what the Englishman is, the steady, plodding worker, without excitement, noise, fuss or nervous exhaustion, just the "pull and get there" in climate and man. In many senses man becomes the atmosphere in which he dwells. As he walks and works, so he looks, and so is he. The Englishman is balanced by his climate. He is not outclassed in mental and physical balance by any nation on earth and to-day that balance in climate, in mental, physical and circumambient atmosphere, will be his ultimate redemption and salvation from the ills that now threaten him on every hand and seem to rise from both earth and ocean.

Every foreign foot that has landed on England this winter has connected with shivers

A WORLD REMAKING

and shakes. Never in twenty-five years has England known such piercing cold, such ice and snow and frost—twenty-five degrees of frost they call it, which means in American vernacular, seven above zero—and never was coal so carefully rationed. You must get a physician's certificate for a fire in your hotel room and you must keep your own internal combustion by carrying your own pocket sugar box.

American travelers borrowed, begged and bribed for hot-water bottles. Lord Timothy Dexter's bed-warming pans which founded his fortune would have been barred out by the coal administrator who rations out to every household its heat units and allows a little free choice and election in the division as betwixt electricity, gas and coal.

The only comfortable people in England this winter were those who commanded peat bogs or wood-piles—no blazing logs, just six-inch billets of hard wood, carefully piecing out your fire.

But cattle throve in the open on dry grass, hay and straw. Pedigreed breeding bulls and registered cows on test in milk production were allowed two pounds of grain a day by government order. The cattle grew warm coats of fur and no native animal—man or brute—complained.

It was just war conditions in continuance, deficient and necessarily-controlled transportation and necessary rationing of food, fuel and shelter; with regulation of all prices, whether butter or beer, rates or rents.

The outsider shivered. He also shook, for the whole frosted island vibrated and shook under the one word "transport."

Transformation is the very foundation of all material civilization. The path and expansion of Roman law, order and organization are marked by the Roman highways.

When London was vibrating between snow and rain, slush, sleet and ice, black fog and black clouds, and sunshine was reckoned only from dates of weeks before, the Underground and Tubes closed down in heartless strike. How the working people got home, or came back to work next morning, nobody seemed to know. The only complaint was in the gentle murmur: "Is this quite fair?"

The transport lorries of the government soon got in their work and took the boys and girls in and out of town in standing-up bunches of fifty as they had moved the workers in France.

A WORLD REMAKING

Then the tubes reopened. The strikers said it was a misunderstanding, but "was it right for the government to interfere in any way with the effectiveness of their strike?"

Still the earth cracked under the threatened strike of the railwaymen for increased wages and the demand of the coal-miners for another raise in pay and shorter hours.

Then the great army of "transport" men ——stevedores, dock men, freight handlers, etc.,—in organized union made their demands. An alliance of the three unions threatened to take control and tie up the island at will and for wages and conditions such as they might elect.

Into Parliament now goes a huge, new bill, called the Transport Bill, proposing a cabinet position and autocratic government therefrom over all the transport of the Kingdom.

Lloyd George vibrates between the Peace Conference and London, and holding Europe, if not the world, in his left hand, he extends the right to his fellow-workmen in Welsh, Scotch and English coal mines and bids them be calm, present their grievances and they shall have justice, whatever it is and whatever it may cost and whoever pays it. The hearing

ENGLAND THE GREAT WAR LOSER

will be short and the decision prompt between the 21st and 31st of March.

When, a few days later in Paris, he stood before me and smiled I was astounded. There was not a wrinkle or a care-line in his face. In a few hours he laid his demand before the Peace Conference and conscription in Germany was doomed. Short of stature he looked to me—he is only a few inches over Napoleon's five feet four—yet, with one hand, he pushes back the threatening internal forces that would disrupt England, and with the other he takes the military sceptre from Germans who may aggregate in the new geographical lines about eighty million people.

How he does it and keeps that smile and full vigor of body and mind, God only knows.

II

WHAT THE PEOPLE OF ENGLAND DO NOT YET KNOW.

ENGLAND, *March, 1919.*

ENGLAND is the great sufferer by the war but not by her human losses—more than three million casualties with a million dead—nor yet by her financial war burden that is expected to stand finally at between thirty-five and forty billion dollars. The 843 bombs that were dropped in England in 108 air raids, that showed the Londoners the bottom of the Thames in daylight, chipped the Embankment and Saint Paul's, failed to explode in front of Westminster Abbey, hit fourteen London banks, killed 1413 people and injured 3407 more and made a map of London look like a peppered paper target, leave no visible scar.

Coal, ships, transportation, the wonderful London discount market and commissions in financing are the foundations of the Empire of England and all these are allied.

WHAT ENGLAND DOES NOT KNOW

Not the German bombs, but war wages and war prices have here made volcanic upheavals.

It can be all summed up in the one word "transport," the power to fetch and carry, to come and go. That sceptre of power, that lance of civilization has been struck down, and it may take more than one Lloyd George to set it up again.

Germany stands, armed cap-a-pie with all her industrial organization and manufactured and stolen machinery, ready to snatch at the commercial prize before Britain can re-organize in transport and rebuild in ships.

The United States, forced by war necessities, is building tonnage faster than Great Britain. And the United States must build quickly for herself and for the world, because England can not alone restore the world's tonnage within a reasonable time.

The English lion of the sea must be argus-eyed, for he must have an eye on Germany and one on America, and a third on Japan. Each of these nations may seek its future on the seas. Each outnumbers Britain in population. Each has the foundation of shipbuilding well-laid. And each has its point of vantage either in machinery, major output per man, low wages, possibilities of government subsidy, possible ambitions, possible necessities in trade and commerce or possibilities in fears concerning national defence.

England built and sold ships at a profit of $40 per ton before the war. Cost per ton of ships has now been multiplied more than three times.

Japan pays her shipbuilders exactly the wages of Belfast and Glasgow. She buys her plates in the United States. Her cost is not ten per cent. higher than Great Britain's per ton of ship, and she has "Pacific" ambitions.

Canada can build ships at $190 per ton and the United States Shipping Board claims a cost not exceeding $225 per ton. But let Uncle Sam *give* the shipyards over to private enterprise and *get out*—note the words "give" and "get out"—and Great Britain, Japan and the United States would all have a cost sheet in shipbuilding at between $130 and $140 a ton.

Don't think for a moment that England can be put out of the game in competition, for at even a construction cost slightly greater than either Japan or the United States, England, with her coal bunkers around the world, her millions of profits from marine insurance, her commissions, financial pickings, and exper-

WHAT ENGLAND DOES NOT KNOW

ience in the multitudinous things that go with shipbuilding and shipsailing, would still be in the running and hold the post of advantage. And the reduced cost in freights might put her back in the industrial race with low cost raw material and low cost for overseas transport of her manufacturers.

But the worst of it is, England's shipping costs are not going down and may go up. Those of Canada and the United States and Japan are likely to come down.

Ask the ordinary Englishman, who is not a shipper, the financial condition of English railways and as he does know that his passenger fare has been advanced 50%, he will tell you that goods rates have probably been advanced and that the government treasury may be sustaining some loss on the railroad guarantees.

But tell him that goods rates have not been advanced during the war and he will not believe you.

Tell him his railroad labor has been increased 130% and steel rails 200% and he will tell you he knows nothing of steel prices, but railroad labor was underpaid and he personally knows that coal has doubled in price.

Tell him that goods rates, or what we call

A WORLD REMAKING

in the States "freight rates," have got to be doubled and he is shocked. He will declare business can not stand it; the government must intervene.

Figure for him how many more hundred miles distant become the colonies of Great Britain by doubling the railroad rates in England and he will be still more astonished.

Push your pencil and pad over to him and ask him to figure whether, economically speaking, South Africa is as formerly 5200 miles distant, or nearer 20,000 miles away from England, when you double English railroad rates, and have normal shipping rates, based upon ships costing three times more than formerly and sailed at a cost of double former wages. The answer finally evoked is that which makes the safety and sanity of the British mind under present conditions: "I'll trust my government and my country to bring this thing out all right."

And the people must trust the government for only the government knows. Less than one thousand people are "in the know" in England and some say less than four hundred.

When somebody publicly asked a cabinet minister what would be the future of the Eng-

WHAT ENGLAND DOES NOT KNOW

lish railways the minister replied: "Nationalization." Then the people asked by what authority he was speaking as the question of railroad nationalization had never been before people or Parliament.

The minister knew the facts and spoke from the facts. He knew that the English railways on the present basis of operating costs could not be handed back to private ownership. They could not be accepted by shareholders or bondholders or be taken by anybody as a gift, because labor and supplies show an operating cost, not of 64% as formerly but of double 64%—indeed somewhere between 130% and 140% for operating expenses alone.

I was discouraged by the condition of the United States railroads under government control, for in January I figured that the government operation of railroads in the United States was costing a billion dollars a year; practically the whole amount the government guaranteed as net return. While the railroads showed seven hundred million of net earnings they had, without expansion of mileage or increased efficiency, borrowed more than seven hundred million during the year. As there had been some increase in locomotive and car equipment, I figured that the American railroads were just about earning their operating expenses. I thought England might teach us something concerning railroad operations, but I found the English railroad system worse off—indeed under water by nearly 30% and the people did not know it.

It took England a year to realize that it had a war on its hands. It will take it a year after the ending of the war to realize that it has peace problems on its hands that may be as great as the war problems.

It was an international war. It is an international wage problem that confronts England, the world and the peace settlements.

England can not stand on her present wage basis unless the wage standard all over the world is advanced.

But how to get England off its war bases and fulfill the political promises that have been made, presents difficulties of no mean proportions.

During the late election there were promises that Germany should pay England's war cost, which were, of course, absurd, unless nobody else was to be paid; that they would hang the Kaiser; that there should be new homes for the people; that the standard of living should

WHAT ENGLAND DOES NOT KNOW

be raised; hours of work should be shortened, etc., etc.

The King opened Parliament the other day expressing the desire that "the *gifts* of leisure and prosperity may be more generally shared throughout the community." Where is the voice to tell the King and his people that leisure and prosperity are the fruit of labor and are never gifts?

England has got to work as she never worked before, not only to pay her war debts, but to recover her position in the business of the world.

The public treasury and the public credit are sustaining practically everything in England. It may be argued that until transportation is normal again England is under the stress of war conditions and her people must be fed and sheltered at the government's expense.

The people write to the papers to know why sugar is bought in Cuba at three times the price at which it is for sale in Java. The answer, of course, is ships. Great Britain can not afford to transport sugar from Java even if it were a free gift in that island. The ocean voyage is too long for the existing shipping conditions. The same response applies when the people want to know why wheat must come from the United States instead of from Australia where it is selling for less than one-half the price in the United States.

The people grumble over the prices for beef and they do not know, for nobody will tell them, that the British treasury has been paying the American packers for beef in New York, transporting it free to England and selling it at retail at the New York price.

When England is at war, the government must supply the food and under present shipping conditions must bring it by the shortest trade routes.

Everything today in England is artificial. The government makes practically every price, every license to import and export and the people must trust their government.

When I asked if I might take home the big volume of data by which the government is subsidizing and regulating trades, supplies, prices, etc., the response was: "You may look at it and that is more than the English public has right to do. It is not intended that the public shall know the conditions. War conditions are still on and until the position is rectified, the people have got to trust us."

Meanwhile the government is selling bread

WHAT ENGLAND DOES NOT KNOW

to the people at 15% to 20% less than cost. Local tramways are maintained at the taxpayers' expense. Rents can not be increased upon the people and the government promise to provide three hundred thousand needed new homes is now met with demand for a million new houses which only the government can build unless rents are doubled.

The telephones are miserably run and the user pays about one fourth the rate paid in the United States. But in England both taxpayers and business suffer. The six-penny telegram that formerly cost the government twelve pence has been advanced to nine pence, but the government treasury fills in the gap.

Of course no such conditions can long endure. England was prepared to continue the war indefinitely, even if she had to fight alone on the sea after Germany had conquered all Europe. Indeed the Englishman would have preferred to sink his island rather than to come under the dominion of the Hun. Instead of fighting for three to five years more, he has this time in which to right himself, restore his shipping, and bring transportation on land and sea again to a sound financial footing.

And the shipbuilders strike and return and

the coal heavers vote to strike and the transport men and the railway men threaten strike.

"Well, we are willing to know the worst and somehow we shall muddle through as we usually do."

"Yes," I responded, "you are willing to know the worst and perhaps you will know it soon enough. You don't know it now. You are the stoutest ally of my country but I believe I can help you to know the worst and that it will help us all at the present time to understand the worst.

"I'll talk to you later about your costs in boots and shoes and machinery, your coal and steel products and the prospective value of the pound sterling."

III

ENGLAND'S WEAKNESS AND RESTRICTED OUTPUT.

LONDON, *March, 1919.*

ONE of the brightest of the English bankers declared to me: "The war changes everything; nothing here, or in this world, will ever again be the same."

The war uncovered the weaknesses of Great Britain in all the foundations of her Empire,— economic, social, political and physical as respects her defences on both land and sea.

The latest revelations of England's physical weakness are to be found in the sensational disclosures of Admiral Jellicoe's new book. It is now shown that while Admiral Beatty with an inferior fleet was smashing away at the Germans off Jutland and calling for Jellicoe to come on, Jellicoe was counting the weaknesses in his armament and measuring the points of advantage held by the German attacking forces. The result now shown was that both Jellicoe and the Germans ran away from each other. Jellicoe says he withdrew a couple of miles fearing to risk an attack with the oncoming darkness and the knowledge that the Germans' shells at the same range could pierce his armorplate while he could not pierce theirs.

His flashlights were inefficient; the Germans had superior carbon points. Jellicoe distrusted both his shells and his ships. He knew that if he failed England was lost. Writers in the press are divided in opinion and some believe that Jellicoe's fears prolonged the war by two years.

There is one thing that England is always ready to concede, and that is any point of outside superiority. She will buy of anybody, anywhere, that will sell her better goods, or give her lower prices. England has grown rich on such a free trade basis as welcomed the dumping upon her of any surplus products from any point of the Globe.

If the United States could refine her nickel more advantageously, it did not matter that the British Empire had all the nickel production, but no refinery. Indeed she was willing to buy a considerable part of her necessary military and naval equipment from Germany and if Germany wished to dump her bounty-

ENGLAND'S DRAWBACKS

fed beet sugar in the English market, closing the English sugar refineries, she was welcome. England would take the German sugar and make marmalade and it is because of this German bounty-fed beet sugar that Tommy in the trenches had to be fed up with marmalade and England had to bid up the price of sugar in Cuba by at least 100%.

Germany is knit together "by orders." England is knit together by precedent and social custom; by "quality" in trade as well as social order, and by that economy, socially and politically recognized which seeks the cheapest market.

England eats marmalade and drinks tea by these fundamental laws in economics and for the most part does not know it. Had English trade and English investments flowed westward to Brazil instead of eastward to India and China, England would never have changed from a coffee-drinking to a tea-drinking people.

England prided herself upon her out-of-door sports, her athletics, her noble specimens of physical manhood. But when it came to the test of war, the English race and all its nobility in blood and manly sons was found endangered because Tommy Atkins from the

A WORLD REMAKING

London streets and the factory towns was physically weak and undeveloped. There is a lesson here from military "rejects," military statistics and hospital reports that England now well understands and is determined measurably to amend. England now knows that her people have been underfed and badly housed and she is determined to amend her social and economic conditions. The declaration of Lloyd George that you can not make an A-1 nation with a C-3 people finds echo in every quarter.

The wages of coal miners and railway employees have been more than doubled by the war and there is nowhere in England a desire that they shall go back a single shilling except in the demonstrated interest of the worker himself and the necessity for marketing and exporting his labor. Indeed the country patiently listens to demands for still further increases in wages and betterment of social and industrial conditions.

The demand in England for protection to the advanced English wages must result in a continuance of the war regulations concerning imports for a long time, unless England determines upon an out-and-out system of American protective tariff duties.

ENGLAND'S DRAWBACKS

It is self-evident that England must import her food and must therefore export the products from her coal mines and factories. If she can not export coal, she must manufacture a great deal more at home and export a great deal more.

There is no way out for her except through increased exports. This means increased production. She has not the machinery to accomplish this and she must demand a larger output per man.

Wages have been so cheap in England that labor-saving machinery has not been invented or invited. If the output fell down, an enlargement of the physical working force was ordered.

England must now be reformed and remade industrially and she faces the situation calmly and with a knowledge that industrial reorganization must be one of the first results from the War. But she as yet little comprehends the size of the problem.

The fetish of the English working man and of his Labor Union has been a restricted output per man upon the theory that diminished production increased the number of jobs. Of course, there could be no reform so long as employers added more hands to keep up the output.

A second fallacy has arisen from the first. And that is that the English climate does not permit quick muscular action; that the lighter sunnier climates, say of the United States, permit increased physical motion; the stimulus of sunshine and the warmer climate requiring a lessened number of meals, etc.

The result is the English workman is encouraged to believe that in his heavy climate he must have his beer and his tea and a bit to eat or drink four to six times a day; that he must be thinking of rest periods, leisure hours and in all his motions, move with deliberation. He must be a "steady" British workman, but never a quick or sprightly, or energized producer.

The economic foundation of England is coal. With coal she not only gives power to her ships, but economic balance to her trade. She exports coal to Argentine, or did before the war, and brings back the cheapest beef. Her ships carried coal for the round trip or could fill from English bunkers in ports around the world. You needed not to leave London to charter your ship and buy her coal supplies around the Globe.

ENGLAND'S DRAWBACKS

But England paid her coal producers an average pre-war wage of 6s 6d per day, or about $1.50. Measured by the day's work in the shift she paid 8s 10d or a little over $2 per day per working coal hand above and under ground. And per man there was never a ton of coal produced, only a fraction of a ton per man.

The war very nearly doubled the wages. The average in November, 1918, was 12s 5d or about $3 per employee and 16s 12d or about $4 per man per shift. But the output per man diminished, due, in part, to poorer quality of employee as men were drawn off for the war, and, in part, to the lengthening distances from the mining shafts, and, in part, no doubt to the labor union heresy of restricted output.

In South Wales the output her employee which had gone down from 269 tons to 243 tons from 1906 to 1913 fell to 224 tons in 1918. In this district labor cost per ton had more than doubled. Supplies had increased in cost per ton from 2s 10d to 8s 10d. But it was the restricted output that troubled the country more than the cost and Lloyd George in the fall of 1918 had to go personally to the coal mining districts and stimulate the output with his inspiring addresses. He told the miners that they were the real fighters against the Huns and that more and more they must "heave coal at them."

When the armistice came there was another effort to increase the coal output, and 200,000 coal miners were given preference in demobilization. Other soldiers protested by riots. Coal was more sharply rationed than ever before in England, and the miners have now demanded a 30% increase in wages and a reduction from eight hours to six hours per day.

A coal commission is now daily taking testimony, receiving volumes of statistics, sifting out the facts, and promises a report before April 1.

If the demand is complied with it will add 9 shillings per ton to the price of coal and this in turn will add 10% to the cost of steel making.

At today's prices, neither coal nor steel can be shipped abroad in competition with the United States, except by government subvention or assistance in transportation.

There are one million men and two hundred thousand boys (under sixteen) and women who draw their wages from coal-mining, and

ENGLAND'S DRAWBACKS

of two hundred and seventy million tons produced in normal times, one hundred million tons go into ships in the proportion of about 25 million tons for bunker coal and 75 million tons for export.

England faces the situation calmly and fully understands that English coal which cost in 1913 eleven shillings per ton at the pit's mouth now costs 18s and will cost not less than 26 shillings if the demands of the miners are granted; and Lloyd George tells Parliament that Pocahontas coal in Virginia, the best that America can produce, is now costing but 11s per ton at the pit's mouth.

How to compete in the future with the United States paying twice the wages, yet producing coal at about one-half the English cost presents many problems. Bunker coal f. o. b. in English ports is costing today 36 to 37 shillings per ton, or about nine dollars. It is of course a controlled commodity, the government naming the price, raking off a profit, and paying not less than 6d per ton as expense of control.

Nevertheless the price of bunker coal f. o. b. at American ports is five dollars, or about 20 shillings per ton. If the government keeps the control, and adds nine shillings or two dollars per ton, the cost of English coal f. o. b. becomes more than double the ship's coal cost per ton in the United States.

Can England put in coal machinery? The answer is that English coal veins run down to 23 inches in width while American coal seams run up to 40 feet in width, and in the United States 16,000 machines cut 253 million tons of coal, while in Great Britain 4000 machines cut only 27 million tons. In many British mines a large part of the day's work is consumed in walking between the shaft and the distant coal face at which he must work.

"Nationalize the mines," cry out the coal miners. Nationalization of coal mines has been a cry in English politics for a generation. It has taken on a new phase of late—a Bolshevik demand in some quarters that as the government wants output, and this is more important than profit, let the government buy the mines and give them to the coal miners, who will run them for output for the public and profit for themselves. The miners say: "We know our own slackers and if we had all the profit we would quickly throw out all the slackers." Thus does Bolshevikism in practice propose to undo the philanthropy of its theories. The main response in England is: "A man in this country shall get what he pays for; stealing is not yet recognized."

There is one sensible suggestion and that is to nationalize the mines by buying out the 1452 coal owners of whom 434 produce less than 2000 tons a year, and, by consolidation of interests and concentrated energies, reduce the expense and enlarge the output. It is thus proposed under the form of a national trust to remove the waste of disjointed ownership.

It would be a singular outcome if England should turn to a trust combination to meet American competition where the economies of combination in trust are forbidden under the Sherman law and the legal decisions superimposed thereupon.

Combination of mines may afford some relief, but confiscation of all the royalties and mining operators' profits would not give one-half the increased wages demanded by the men. Royalties are about 6d per ton and the pre-war profits per ton were only 1s. The coal operators' profits have been expanded during the war to 3s 6½d. But of the 60 cents per ton increase the government in excess profits and income taxes takes the major part.

As near as can be estimated the total capital

A WORLD REMAKING

in the English coal industry, not including freehold realty, is 128 million pounds sterling.

The British official record shows that in 1916 the worker in the United States produced 896 tons of soft coal per annum, and in anthracite mines, 548 tons of coal per annum. This compares with 207 tons of anthracite per man per annum in the mines of South Wales and only 222 tons of soft coal per man per annum in South Wales.

The comparison shows more than four tons of soft coal for the American worker as compared with one ton of soft coal for the English worker. Many mines in the United States have a much higher production per man, but the average English production in soft coal ranges from 230 to 260 tons per man per annum.

The coal hearing occupies a page or two in the daily press. But neither from the hearing nor the press will you learn the supreme and controlling fact and factor, if there is to be an international coal situation.

Please don't ask me where I get the fact or the figures, for they are not in the possession of any government and they cost too much money to be otherwise than privately controlled.

ENGLAND'S DRAWBACKS

But the fact is that in normal times the United States has a 20% surplus coal capacity. Now as the production in the United States is twice that of Great Britain, the United States has normally a surplus coal capacity that is 40% of the strained and maximum coal capacity of Great Britain.

P. S.: The coal commission has made majority report which has been accepted by the Government in favor of seven hours for underground work instead of eight, from July 16, and six hours from July 13, 1921, subject to the economic position of the industries; also an increase of two shillings per shift for colliery workers and an advance of one shilling for workers under 16 years. The report condemns present system of ownership and working and will report by May 20 on questions of nationalization or unification by national purchase or joint control. This means the continuance of coal control for two years.

IV

Costs For Steel And Thought.

London, March, 1919.

THE most surprising statement made to me in London was that the United States could lay down steel in South America cheaper than England could put it on board ship in her own ports; and this notwithstanding the abnormal freights now prevailing on the ocean. The statement was so astonishing that I must quote it exactly as made by an English director of railways in England, India and South America. He said:

"India, Brazil and Argentina are crying out for steel, but the best England can do is £17 a ton f. o. b., or $85 per ton, against £12, or $60 per ton f. o. b. in the United States. The United States can deliver steel into Argentina below the price in Great Britain."

This statement was so astounding that I went elsewhere for explanation and called upon another business friend, registered likewise in

COSTS FOR STEEL AND THOUGHT

the books with the title "Sir" before his name. He said:

"Yes, the price quoted for steel for export is correct. We cannot, under present circumstances, do it for less. One-third of our iron ore is hematite from Sweden, Norway and Spain. It was 8 shillings before the war boomed the freight rates. It was 80 shillings per ton during the war, and now it is 60 shillings per ton.

"As we must use a certain percentage of imported hematite, the shipping situation largely raises our costs. Prices are all fixed by the government, both for domestic consumption and for export.

"The government still furnishes the ships for the import of the ore and the export of steel.

"There is a government subsidy of an average of £4 per ton, but it is not all direct. Part of it is in freights.

"The situation may be illustrated by steel plates, the price of which is fixed by the government at £11 10s. for home consumption, but £19 per ton for export. The government, however, is soon to put down the export price to £15, or $75 per ton."

A WORLD REMAKING

Then I went to another man interested in shipping, and he said:

"The government brings in the hematite ore from Spain at about 45 shillings in charter boats taken over early in the war at the control, or Blue Book rate of 11½ to 12½ shillings per ton. As it pays several times Blue Book rates for neutral tonnage, the government has the right to average out its freight rates as it pleases. There would be no sense in paying neutral countries high freight rates and shipping them products at prices lowered by commandeered home tonnage."

Representatives of Canadian shipbuilding and iron and steel interests were in London, and I was astonished to learn from these that Canada can not produce rails at the price named in the United States, $57 per ton. The United States Railroad Administration has recently asked Canada a price on rails, but Canada cannot give it because the quotation of $57 in the United States is below Canadian costs, when all depreciation and overhead charges are taken into consideration.

The Canadian government contract with the Dominion Iron & Steel Corporation, under

COSTS FOR STEEL AND THOUGHT

which the latter is building its plate mill, calls for a price of $83 per ton for plates.

Canada, however, is going forward in shipbuilding and railroad upbuilding and is developing a spirit of independence toward the mother country.

There are large unsettled accounts between England and Canada, which may cause friction. Canada loyally surrendered her ships to Great Britain, but now most imperially demands back all the profits Great Britain has made by carrying Canadian troops in these Canadian-owned ships.

The Canadians declare emphatically that they do not care to be signatories to any League of Nations; that they do not want to be tied up too closely with the British Empire in the political affairs of Europe.

Canada fought loyally for the Empire, but now finds Great Britain treats Canada in many respects as a foreign or neutral country. It is selling government ships to British citizens at $100 per ton, but outside countries, including Canada, can not have them for less than $200 per ton. Of course, the answer is that Great Britain can afford to sell her government ships to British citizens who will return her a large portion of the present high

A WORLD REMAKING

freight rates in excess profit taxes and income taxes.

Nevertheless Canada does not quite understand that it is a great privilege for her citizens to apply for license to send into England one-quarter of what she exported to England in 1914, which, of course, means, as 1914 was only a half year, one-eighth.

The most important economic factor in Great Britain at the present time is that wages have been almost universally doubled by the war, and that there will be a universal effort to maintain them so long as economic conditions warrant—and possibly longer.

Farm hands got 16 shillings per week before the war. Now they are receiving 40 shillings per week, and the government guarantees a minimum wage of 30 shillings.

The wages of English seamen were raised during the war from £6 a month to £11, and to this was added a war bonus of £3, which is expected to drop off when peace is signed.

Wages were raised in the engineering trades. The government on Jan. 1 last reduced the hours of work from 54 to 47, and at the same time gave an increase of 5 shillings per week. Manufacturers had a three weeks' notice of this, but it was largely ignored in the papers.

COSTS FOR STEEL AND THOUGHT

Indeed, one might be in England for many weeks, and so far as the newspapers are concerned would learn little of the industrial changes which are going on at the foundations of the Empire.

It has just been figured out that engineering or machinists' wages have increased in England during the war by 126% from a pre-war basis of 43 shillings 6d. per week. First, the government added a war bonus of 5 shillings a week; then another 5 shillings; later a 12½% increase on the whole; then several more 5 shilling bonuses so that the total is now 98 shillings 6d. The Vickers people and press manufacturers agree that the war bonuses will stand, but it may be possible to cut off the 12½% increase. This is the most that can be expected in reduction of wages in what would be called in the United States machinist's lines, but in England is known as the engineering trades.

The result is that American printing presses and typesetting machines can be built in the United States 10% cheaper than in England. It is everywhere, however, confessed that English wages before the war were on a starvation basis.

A WORLD REMAKING

The question now remaining is: Can England change her methods and put in machinery for more economical production?

Investigators of this situation are in doubt as to whether there is not great trouble ahead of England before she can get upon the American basis of enlarged output per man.

In England the working men are thoroughly wedded to their system of restricted output. In New York one man will run three gear-cutting machines, but an English-working man will run only one.

In clerical forces there is the same redundancy of labor—nearly a double staff everywhere. Carbon-copies are not legal in England and everything has to be letter-pressed.

One improvement has been made in shipping by raising the Plimsoll waterline mark 14 to 18 inches during the war, thus greatly increasing ships' capacity. This was also found advantageous in making a lower visibility during the war. In some cases ships have now only 4½ foot free board.

One of the bright international shipping men tells me that it is more terminal machinery that is needed over the world rather than more ships' tonnage.

When a boat load of iron ore arrives in

COSTS FOR STEEL AND THOUGHT

Great Britain eight days are consumed in unloading it. On the Great Lakes in America, if the same tonnage was not unloaded in eight hours, the wires would be kept hot with inquiries.

The conditions that are now pressing home on England and the whole world are causing an awakening—an awakening to the value of thought and invention—the work of the expert.

The day of brag and bluster has gone. Press and Politics are bidding for the men who can think. The sound editorial, the enlightening communicated article, the work of the reviewer are all again to the front.

News of thought here in England is now more important in the daily press than ever before.

Not long ago, the important question was: "How much money have you got?"

But, now, the question is being forcefully asked: "How did you get it?"

England has been a nation of middlemen and brokers. The world has paid her commissions. But the people of England are now beginning to ask if they, themselves, have not been paying too many and too high commissions in some services. Are there not too many who "do nothing but chip a bit off the values of things as they pass?"

"Service and Reward" are under discussion as never before. I have before me a whole newspaper page containing portraits of ten living authors or men in the public eye, and there are eighteen articles in about forty paragraphs, expressing the individual opinion of these and other leaders in English thought, presenting "Today's views on subjects topical."

An inventor says: "One of my patents is now saving the world eight to ten million pounds every year. And yet my own return on this was a comparatively small sum. Our patent laws, instead of encouraging inventive genius, have done their best to stifle it. It is difficult to calculate the loss to the country by this grudging attitude toward the inventor."

One warns labor and the trade union that "the country is sick to death of the Prussian methods."

Another declares: "I can see nothing else, for the moment, than to solve the housing problem by commandeering some of the larger houses and turning them into flats."

Another asks: "Can labor control?" And answers: "One of the fundamental differ-

COSTS FOR STEEL AND THOUGHT

ences between labor and capital is that labor can quit a job, but capital cannot.''

Canon Adderley is quoted in favor of ''a brighter Sunday'' in which bishops have Sunday afternoon fetes and invite the Trade Unions with their families.

The most singular thing in all this presentation of modern thought is the call of the economist to fight bankruptcy and Bolshevism by larger production, while the production of babies, from every angle, seems to baffle all the thinkers.

The Bishop of Birmingham points out that while the birth-rate is falling there is no diminution in the size of the poorer families who give birth to babies they cannot afford to keep, while ''the better class people'' are ceasing to have children at all. ''Whether the State should undertake the care of our poor children, is a question for our statesmen to answer.'' Another writer advocates the prevention of marriage among ''those unable to breed healthy children and let there be no bones about it. Society is entitled to protect itself, but before it can do so, it must away with sickly sentiment and parsons' slop; otherwise it will be so bitten by the serpent bred of its own neglect that its existence may well be in

A WORLD REMAKING

danger. In other words, if civilization is to protect itself, it must be as ruthless as Nature."

The questions of divorce, of marriage responsibilities, of duties to children and duties to the State are under discussion as never before.

Nobody seems to understand the higher law or to be able to put clearly the case of man the highest product of the Creator.

Lady Tree writes on "The Eternal Duo" and boldly declares that, "beyond the function of motherhood, man does everything better than woman; that she must fulfill that function and must be content to leave the economic and political struggle to man." As a worker with wounded men in the hospitals, she declares: "In so essentially feminine a thing as needle-work, men beat women hollow. The work of the world is best done by men. Genius is beyond all rules, but if I were advising a girl what to do to become a good actress, I should advise her to watch and study actors, not actresses.

"Meanwhile, women themselves are wearying of the supposed delights of independence which has spoilt their manners and the manners of men as a consequence. And they are

COSTS FOR STEEL AND THOUGHT

inclining to love and to motherhood and the indulgence of that feeling of satisfaction which all true women feel in relying on a man and having a man to rely on.''

All of which shows that there is a great popular demand for thought and a lot of dangerous thought awaiting the clarifying influence of the highest ideals.

The war has awakened the thought of the world. It is not, for a moment, to be assumed that people, at the beginning, are going to think straight, clear or true. But, best of all, they are beginning to think.

The printing press is turning out books on the "awakening of Asia" and on the "awakening of India." It is declared "that India, like Japan and China, is awakening."

People are thinking concerning economics, popular sanitation and popular education.

Whereas it was once felt that men had a right to life, but no inherited right on land or water, it is now no heresy to declare that man has right to be born right, to be fed aright, to be trained aright, to be educated aright, and that then he has "right to liberty and the pursuit of happiness."

It is also beginning to be admitted that he has some right, not only in a common fatherhood, but a common brotherhood and may enter somewhat into the accumulated inheritances.

V

Ships And Shipping.

London, March, 1919.

THE international problem is not trade but ships. There can be no normal international trade until the shipping situation is again normal.

England was alarmed when she saw the United States with her giant resources launching a program that gave promise of a million new tons of ships every month. She knew that her Empire was based, not upon an ocean of water, but an ocean of ships and shipping.

In London last year I was called upon to tell the shipping people most emphatically that while the United States had the potential capacity to build a million tons per month, or twelve million ship tons per annum in defending European and American civilization, it had no shipping program beyond that of the defences of war; that it was building every kind of a barge, boat, ship or steamer that

A WORLD REMAKING

could be floated with wood, steel, or cement and it was building to feed its allies and to put the boys in khaki over the ocean by the million; that when Judge Gary of the United States Steel Corporation declared at a public reception to the Embassy from Japan, that the United States could put fifteen million men into the war and a hundred billions of credit behind them, he was talking truth, but we would have to build our own ships to do it, for the allies could not fight their defensive warfare and also build the ships for us.

But, as for any mercantile shipping program, I told them we had it not, and nobody could tell whether two years after the war the United States government would own a single ship, although if the war lasted long enough and it was necessary, we would duplicate the entire maximum pre-war world shipping of forty-eight million tons.

Now England views the international shipping situation with more equanimity. With the armistice and prospective closing of the war, she sees her maximum shipbuilding capacity of 2,500,000 tons per annum restored and she likewise sees the American estimates that rose as high as twelve million tons per annum, cut to three million tons as maximum. The practical English shipping people tell me that for effective ocean-going carrying capacity, the United States will in this year turn out nearer one million tons than two million tons.

England also now sees more clearly that our ships were built for the war, and not to displace English shipping by bountyfed ships sustained by the United States Treasury and income taxes. England also sees the necessarily poor quality of our ship construction and understands very well that the commercial shipping turned out by the United States government was largely from construction started in private shipyards and taken over by the government.

England has also counted up her own resources. Her American compatriots in Canada have frankly told her that it would be many years before Canada could approach English shipbuilding costs except in some lines of cheap freighters.

As to big ocean liners, of which the world now stands in such need for troop transportation and passenger and express service, only England and Germany can build such ships in the near future.

A WORLD REMAKING

The Belfast shipbuilder is a trained workman; trained to the extent that 240 of him need only one boss, or overseer. But in Canada, it is confessed, a superintendent is needed over every sixteen men.

Stand on the deck of a European liner—the Mauretania, 790 feet long with 45,000 tons displacement and 67,000 horse power, or the Olympic just under 900 feet, or the Aquitania, 902 feet, with 55,000 tons displacement and 60,000 horsepower,—and if you will step on a few inches of brass plates, that most passengers never notice, although there are three of them crossing the ship, you may feel the ship bend at these points, and separate by a half inch right under your feet, for that is where the ship opens and closes as she rises and falls.

Go down to your cabin, luxuriously lined in oak or maple and you will not find a bit of joiner work started or cracked, nor hear a single wood strain. That joiner work is put together in such a manner by ship experts as not to be unmade by the strains in the ship. No ordinary housebuilder or carpenter can do such interior ship fitting.

It can be readily imagined that such trades have run from father to son in Glasgow and

SHIPS AND SHIPPING

Belfast since the Britannia of 1840, the first Cunarder, was launched to surprise the ocean as it displaced 1154 tons of water and brought its 207 feet of ship-length over to Boston harbor with a horsepower of just 740, or slightly more than 1% of the horsepower that sent the Aquitania down the narrow Clyde in April, 1914, and on her war career of south Atlantic cruiser, Gallipoli transport, hospital ship for the Mediterranean, then overseas troopship with 7000 American boys and now soon to go back into first-class passenger service.

A ship like the Aquitania that never varies 30 minutes in her scheduled translantic voyage of five days and five hours is not the product of one generation, but of at least three generations of training in engineering skill and labor organization.

Yet today the Belfast shipbuilder has an average wage of $17 per week. In British parlance tradesmen average 78 shillings and workmen 57 shillings per week in the Belfast yards.

If the United States could turn her steel and timber into giant quantities of shipbuilding and sell to the stars, she might do in ships what she has done in shoes and coal, pay double wages and halve the English cost

A WORLD REMAKING

by reason of the output being two and a half to four times the English output per man.

But shipbuilding is more a product of handicraft than of machinery with quantity output.

It is stability in labor, trade, service and output that gives value to English production.

No revolutionary country, or country of sudden or sweeping changes could enter into the fruitage of England's steady trade.

There is stability about England possessed by no other country in the world. Everywhere there is apology made me for the temporary character of the hotel service. "The regular valet will soon be back, sir."

"Thank you," you answer, and the next week you are surprised to be again informed by James: "I am going, sir, tomorrow. I was here only temporary. The regular man has returned and he will do everything all right, sir."

"How long have you been here temporarily?" you ask, in some resentment that weekly or monthly changes of servants should be your concern.

The response is: "Oh, only four and a half years. The regular man has been away in the war."

What would one think of that for a tempo-

SHIPS AND SHIPPING

rary position in the United States? If you want to contemplate temporary situations, cast your eye down toward Panama, or Mexico, where revolutions, the last hundred years, have been measured by months instead of years.

And still the question facing England is as to whether her labor is now in a state of revolution, or "just temporary, sir!" Present wages are revolutionary as compared with the past and their future is dependent upon a world situation. The shipping situation throws a wall of protection about England, as did the war wall about the United States when American industries were sinking in 1914.

England has done the shipbuilding of the world and for the same reason that her bunkers have coaled the world's shipping—because she has done it steadily and cheaper. But it will be a long time before England, if ever, gets back to a pre-war basis of cost.

In shipping there are two factors that will maintain high shipping rates for a long time. People who have looked for normal ocean freight rates this summer, are reckoning without a knowledge of the factors in the situation. It is an old saying that nothing will lie like statistics. The truth of this arises from the fact that statistics usually give measure of only one factor when there are many factors entering into the problem.

Statistics show that the world is three million tons short in shipping. There are two other factors they do not show. The first is that the war demand on shipping, to undo what it took more than four years to build up, will last through 1920. The second is that the three million ton absence in ships does not accurately measure the tonnage shortage.

The shipping of the world is worn out and boats that go into dock for repairs will not come out for six months. This is the information I have from shipping people here who sail ships on both sides of the Atlantic.

The ship repair facilities of the world will be strained for more than one year. A three-million-ton shortage in ships today, may, with the worn-out condition of the ships represent more than a six-million-ton shortage.

In England there are docking facilities and repair yards for every 95,000 tons of shipping. Shipping people figure that a repair yard is required for every 100,000 tons in service. It will thus be seen that in the repair work England has a margin of only 5%, and England is the repair yard of the world.

SHIPS AND SHIPPING

If the United States is to go into any extensive shipbuilding, coupled with future ship-repairing and ship-sailing, it must not only repeal the LaFollette act, but launch its labor and capital and engineering talent upon an extensive system of docks and repair yards.

American talent and American capital can be better invested in the long run; but building of ships must go on in the United States because, as a protective measure inaugurated by the war, it must be continued until the demands caused by the war have been satisfied and England is again able to supply the world's shipping requirements upon a lower basis than the United States.

Before the war, an average of two million tons of English shipbuilding sufficed for the world's demands. The United States can raise tea in South Carolina; and California raises a good staple cotton, but cotton pays better than tea in South Carolina and oranges pay better than cotton in California. Nevertheless, if disaster should put the South out of the cotton business for a time, the United States might have to raise cotton in California and if the Orient were to be cut off for some years from the United States tea might

A WORLD REMAKING

be forced, as a necessary but temporary exotic, in the Carolinas.

Ships are necessary in the world's commerce and the disaster of war makes it necessary that the United States co-operate for some years in their replacement. But with peace in the world, there is no economic necessity for any large United States shipbuilding program.

So long as New England supplied at low rate the western railroad capital the prosperous farmer of Kansas and Iowa would have been foolish to attempt railroad construction when hogs, corn and wheat paid so much better.

Although England began early to commandeer her ships, taking 2200 into the government service in the first few months of the war, there were vast shipping interests in other countries, somewhat English-owned, that could not be commandeered, and English shipping men have piled up fortunes equalling those war-made profits of the French motor makers and the munition people in the English Midlands.

Shipping fortunes have been made around the world in the operation and the overturn of ships. But, when three to five years from now, the demands made by the war and the readjustments following the war are over, there may be a long period in which the owners of coal-burning ships will be in despair not only for cargoes, but for values.

Coal-burning ships for both war and peace are doomed if the oil supplies of the world hold out and expand as now promised. But this is another story and one of vital importance and must await another article. Suffice it to say, at the present time, that the United States on a commercial basis should stick to its field in competitive building of electrical apparatus, electrical equipment and small engines for ships.

A shipping man tells me that he went looking for ship engines a few weeks ago and a price of $80,000 was named by a leading English firm. He said he could get the engines for $78,000 in the States. The English firm replied: "Name any reasonable sum. We want the business."

However, he did not have to wait. A bid of $63,000 came from the United States and took the order.

VI

ENGLISH SHIPPING AND RAILROADS.

LONDON, *March, 1919.*

UNLESS the United States uses its Treasury and taxing powers to strike at the shipbuilding and shipping situation of her war ally, Great Britain, England can well defend herself for many years against all other comers in shipping on the present national and international wage scale.

It is in her coal, iron, steel and railroad transportation that she is in greatest economic danger.

The total exports of coal from the United Kingdom in 1913 were nearly 75,000,000 tons and represented three-fourths of the total weight of exports of all kinds. If the bunker coal placed in foreign-going vessels be added, the amount of coal would be nearly 100,000,000 tons or one-third of the output of the United Kingdom and more than 10% of the total value of all the exports, about $250,000,000 in an export of less than $2,500,000,000.

In the twenty years preceding the war, England's exports had doubled, but her imports had increased only 60% to $3,500,000,000. The statistics of England's foreign trade dispute the contention of Germany that England was jealous of Germany's expansion—which Germany calls her kultur—and secretly promoted the war to ruin Germany. The trade of the United Kingdom with Germany, Austria and Turkey was of the most regular character, averaging around 11½% of the United Kingdom's foreign trade, the larger part of which was, of course, with Germany, and exports and imports with that country were never 10% of Britain's trade.

It was in the steel trade that England failed to advance and here she had more right to be jealous of the United States than of Germany. England's steel production rose from 6,500,000 tons in 1906 to 7,700,000 tons in 1913, while Germany increased from 11,100,000 tons to 18,700,000 and the United States from 23,400,000 tons to 31,300,000 tons.

In exports of iron and steel, England's values went from £41,000,000 in 1906 to £55,000,000 in 1913, while Germany advanced

A WORLD REMAKING

from £28,000,000 to £54,000,000 or nearly double, and the United States' exports of iron and steel went in the same time from £15,000,000 to £32,000,000, or more than double, and the United States was not seriously in the field before 1900.

The United States Steel Corporation started with a greater output than that of all Great Britain. English capital has since been steadily avoiding British iron and steel industries. Indeed, the government has long had under consideration the question of anti-dumping legislation and the imposition of custom duties to protect British iron and steel industries.

The trouble is that, like coal, British steel is important to British ships and shipping, which are the defences of England and her trade.

For the ten years preceding the war, England's shipbuilding held fairly constant at 61% of the world's output.

There are very nearly 500,000 working people employed on the railroads in England including engineers, stationmasters, trainmen, etc. The standard payment, before the war, was 25 shillings per week, but with over time at 25% extra—they now ask double pay for overtime—the earnings averaged 28s 6d per

ENGLISH SHIPPING AND RAILROADS

week for all the working force, exclusive of counsel, salaried officials and clerical forces.

With the war bonus, wages are now up to 67 shillings per week with average for the past year at about 61 shillings 6 pence. The estimated number of men employed by the railroads in July, 1914, was just over 650,000. Last April there were 116,000 fewer men and 53,000 more women, a reduction in the total force of 63,000.

During the war, trains were consolidated, all unprofitable work was eliminated and passenger rates were increased 50% in order to diminish travel. But the war workers had the money to spend and the English people would not give up their week-ends. It is doubtful if the passenger business really diminished. The increased rate did not apply to workmen's tickets, and season tickets got only 10% to 20% increase.

As the ordinary passenger fares in 1913 were £50,500,000 and the season tickets £5,000,000, the increase in passenger rates may be estimated at £20,000,000. This with the added facilities of the government during the war and the reduction in trains and employees, is all there is to offset the increased wages and increased cost of material in operation.

A WORLD REMAKING

Total passenger receipts before the war, including parcels on passenger trains and working men's tickets were £57,000,000 per annum. The receipts from freight or goods traffic were £66,500,000, a total of £124,000,000.

The operating basis was 64%

Today, the increased cost of materials is £20,000,000; the increased cost of wages £60,000,000 and the eight-hour day just inaugurated will add £12,000,000, a total of £92,000,000 additional expense, where before the war there was only £124,000,000 of gross receipts.

The war bonus, which I have included in the above figures of wages, was 15 shillings at the beginning of 1917, 21 shillings at the end and was advanced to 33 shillings only in 1918. Women got one-half the bonus and eventually up to 20 shillings. Now they are gradually going out of the service.

The cost of operating the railroads before the war was about £79,000,000. Today the operating expenses must be about £175,000,000.

With the operating deficit and the guaranties of interest and dividends, the deficit upon the British treasury must be now nearly £75,000,000 per annum. No figures are published nor is the gross or net return of any individual railroad publicly known.

ENGLISH SHIPPING AND RAILROADS

I thought when I left the States in January, there was behind me a problem in transportation of giant proportions. I was astonished to find a larger one here.

The difference between the two is that Washington has listened to political expediency and has unnecessarily increased railroad wages from typewriters to station agents, while England has necessarily used her railroads in vast war machinery, has increased wages as necessary war measures and has not had time to make the readjustments.

Great Britain had the best of the railroad bargain at first, with the large increase in government traffic, and had no necessity to keep financial accounts in movement of troops or munitions. Goods rates have not been advanced, as an advance was not necessary at first. The government traffic was enormous and the advance in operating expense was not onerous until about a year ago.

The government's guaranties and control run for two years after the ratification of the Treaty of Peace.

It is realized that an advance in railroad rates will be a very serious matter for English commerce and exports.

Although Lloyd George has stated in Par-

A WORLD REMAKING

liament the increased cost of operation as about £90,000,000, nobody seems to pay any attention to it. Railroad shareholders come together in annual meeting and receive the felicitations of the chairman upon an extra dividend as though the extra dividend came from the traffic and the business end of the concern, when in reality it comes from accumulations and sinking funds and undivided surpluses in the treasury added to the government rental or guaranty.

However the calm view in England must be that the war is still on and that for two years after peace is declared there must be war readjustments which are legitimately the capital expenditures and losses of war.

The English view is always at long range. It is not what happened yesterday or is to arrive tomorrow but what was the situation with the family and the State a generation ago and what it should be a generation hence; there is a lesson in the history of the past and there is a history ahead; but a few years more or less between times for planning and engineering do not matter.

"It was twenty-six years ago," said a railroad employe to me, "that we began to look up in our trade. Then 'railroad servants' became 'railroad men' and wages were 16 shillings a week. Now they are over 60 shillings and they are going to stay up and conditions are going to be improved."

That is the fundamental and the labor side.

The financial side is this—from headquarters in the railroad and financial world,—but subject always to any necessary variation:

"We shall have a director of transportation. He will name rates, wages and conditions and the government will back him up. There will be an advance in goods rates, but we think it ought not to be as much as 50%. Then rates will be adjusted so as to let in raw materials at low cost and encourage the export trade. But there will be a kind of protection against foreign imports of manufactured goods. This is the plan."

VII

The Value of the Pound Sterling

LONDON, *March, 1919.*

I WAS surprised to have the question put up to me so often in February by English financiers and economists: "How will the United States deal with our indebtedness to her Treasury; how soon will she ask payment?"

I always responded with a laugh that Uncle Sam's loans to John Bull were a war measure; a bond of alliance in mutual defence against the common enemy. We expected the interest to be paid promptly, but we had no thought concerning a day for the payment of the principal. It was absurd to consider that question now.

The reply was: "We are in your debt; at your mercy; you could embarrass us by calling for payment."

I said the question was not discussable. The United States could not embarrass a fellow

THE VALUE OF THE POUND STERLING

fighter even with discussion of the due date; that the only question that had been discussed in the United States was whether we might not some time consider the sacrifices of France in defence against the common enemy and cancel the obligations, in whole or in part, behind the two and a half billion which had been advanced to her. But I thought that all the Allies would prefer to pay their indebtedness, as in the end the best security and bond of union for the future. It might be many years before we would suggest any payment of principal, or due date so long as a fair rate of interest was paid.

It was not until this month that I came to the conclusion that there was a bigger question in the background that English finance did not desire to discuss too openly.

I did not understand until this month that the United States Treasury had been sustaining the exchanges of the world.

When we began advancing money to our allies, it was stated that it was to cover purchases in the States. It had occurred to me that the money was going out rather more rapidly than orders were coming in; indeed that the money was flowing out rather in inverse ratio to incoming orders for ordnance or goods.

"What is the difference——" said a United States Treasury official to me on this side of the water, "what is the difference which kind of orders we cash? We owe for transportation of troops and buy on account heavily abroad. We loan to each other supplies and munitions of war. International exchange is one of the great factors in the war. We are all in the exchange market, and the supply market and support each other in the common end of winning the war. You can not divide the accounts and we must sustain, to the limit of the appropriation, our allies' foods and supplies, as well as their fighting men, and this means sustenance in credit. It is true that nine-tenths of the appropriation of ten billion has been taken and there is only a billion left."

That was really the problem behind the interrogatories fired at me.

How long would international credit be sustained by the United States Treasury, and when Uncle Sam's support was removed what would be the value of the pound sterling and the French franc?

More and more it comes to be openly discussed that the peg must be withdrawn and

THE VALUE OF THE POUND STERLING

the pound sterling must seek its level in the world's markets.

With their usual brutal frankness over an unpleasant situation, there is a boldness of English sentiment which says: "Let the worst be known. Pull out the peg. Let the pound sterling go to $4.00, $3.75, or even $3.50. The lower it goes, the more trade will be turned toward the Empire of Britain."

It is in preparation for a trade, rather than a treasury sustenance, that England is now issuing orders-in-council prohibiting certain foreign purchases, is granting limited trade licenses and is holding government control upon all lines of shipping, of trade and of transport.

There is also another feature, one that no one would have dared suggest a few years ago to a Briton—a necessary inflation, with a necessary temporary abandonment of the gold standard. And this somewhat in order to meet the rising demands of labor. England looks well ahead. She has the foresight of the southern colored economist who declared: "Yo 'ere niggahs what doan' like de silba dollah fo' de whitewash work, kain jes, take de papah dollah, shoah."

England is preparing for self-protection in

A WORLD REMAKING

many ways. Nobody expects Bolshevik trouble in England, but carefully chosen regiments are called home and the Guards are drilled, I know, quietly concerning the handling of crowds, attempted disturbances and in the meaning of the riot act.

England is also counting up her gold reserves that are not yet mobilized under the Bank of England. One bank has forty million dollars of gold in its vaults and the question has been discussed as to whether the scattered gold in joint stock banks had not better be under the Bank of England reserve where it counts in weekly reports around the world, rather than practically lost as a credit support in miscellaneous bank reserve items.

Would it not be better for English trade that the gold reserve in the Bank of England show above 25% rather than under 20%?

Some of the bankers are insistent that every effort must be made to sustain English credits and the value of the pound sterling and that the way to do it is to give full banking credit to merchants who desire to ship in security and safety, goods to foreign parts, to Italy, Roumania and the East so far as transportation can be secured.

English banking credit, they declare, is the

best sustainer of English trade and of the pound sterling. And the English trade ship is well-manned, fore and aft, and not a pulley will be missed in holding English trade.

No longer may an advancing Bank of England rate draw money from the ends of the earth, or from the moon, for England is no longer the greater creditor nation, controlling money and affecting trade by the rate of interest at the world's financial center.

I am told in the financial district that England owes not alone the $4,000,000,000 due to Uncle Sam's treasury but altogether nearer $20,000,000,000.

Today the Bank rate is 5%; the discount rate is $3\frac{1}{2}\%$ in the open market and yet $4\frac{1}{4}\%$ is paid on deposits by the large joint stock banks. It is by this high rate on deposits, paid to special interests, that money is attracted to the City, the discount rate on international bills is kept down and England is defended as an international money center.

VIII

England's Protection Policy

LONDON, *March, 1919.*

THE eight million people that still hold the center of the stage in war, peace, finance and problems of civilization and are counted as London, divide into many cities and in a sense every part is a foreign part.

Thousands daily work in "the City" or financial district and know nothing of the West End or Westminster. But in the halls of Westminster, the representative of "the City" has been there for a generation and what is going on in Parliamentary circles, at the Treasury, and before the Cabinet, is closely followed by the leaders in finance. Although England recognizes the rising power of the Labor Party, the foundations of the Empire, in finance and in trade, are nowhere attacked as in the United States.

The Englishman is for law and order every time, although he will patiently listen to all sorts of proposals to improve the conditions of labor and join in demands for better housing conditions and better industrial conditions.

Indeed there is a stronger and more universal sentiment in England today for improved conditions of labor than one hundred years ago when Robert Owen stood before Parliament and demanded reforms for the poor and the down-trodden in England's industrial system, when babes went from the workhouse to labor in practical servitude at five years of age, and the English agricultural laborer was little better than a serf.

Everybody now sees more clearly that a nation exists in its people and not in its wealth, and there is a better understanding of the American protective system which has raised the wages of labor and protected "the home market" in which labor spends its higher wages, and effects a broad general prosperity to the despair of the theoretical free trader.

The protection that the United States formerly threw around labor, the British government is today throwing around finance and the protection of her "City" interests. It is to protect finance, the value of the pound sterling, the gold basis of England, and maintain her international discount market that England's decrees go forth limiting imports.

It is not that England would not like the goods at low prices. It is not that England would protect her home market. It is that England must protect her financial base.

England is not attempting to protect the labor of the hundreds of bill brokers who still wear their top hats in the "City" summer and winter and eat their noon luncheon on the same spot and at the same minute as for twenty years past. England is endeavoring to protect that trade which is the bulwark of the island and whose shipways between foreign ports and English warehouses are greased from the English discount market. The simplicity of the machinery here is hieroglyphic to the outside world. The strongest endorsement is "eminently respectable." The strongest condemnation is "look sharp."

Every man selects his bills for the investment of surplus funds and is never asked why he buys a certain line and always rejects a certain other line. Whenever there is a dereliction in the City, a piece of sharp practice, it is never forgotten or forgiven; however high the tide of fortune may rise.

There is one thing that makes the "City"

ENGLAND'S PROTECTION POLICY

man warm under the collar at the present time and that is the quotation at about 82 of the 3% Exchequer bonds due in 1930. They quote them in the "City" by the name of "Swindles."

England has stood behind English exchanges and war credits. When the Russian treasury bills, nine million pounds sterling, became due a year ago, the British government, which had asked the "City" folks originally to grant this credit, concluded it could not allow a default, but that it could propose a compromise.

It gave the holders the 3% Exchequer bonds. Altogether there was fifteen million pounds sterling in the transaction and the "City" men exclaimed: "The Government could give five hundred million sterling for munitions, but to save three million, it spoiled the market. Compromise is a swindle, and what is offered to us now—just swindles."

And "Swindles" they became in the parlance of the "City."

One realizes the unity and power of Great Britain when in distant quarters he hears the command: "British subjects pass this way" and it is obeyed quietly and without question. The Englishman is proud of the words "Brit-

A WORLD REMAKING

ish" and "subjects." The man from America may proclaim himself a citizen, but will deny that he is a subject to anything under Heaven. Yet there can be no nation and no citizenship unless all citizens are subjects under the law.

Orders are still given and executed in England with a quietness that is astonishing.

An American friend of mine noticed in the elevators connecting with the Underground Railways the "No Smoking" sign; penalty 40 shillings. He was astonished to see pipes, cigars and cigarettes in the mouths of the people in the elevators, and pointed out the situation to his English friend as an evidence of England's falling away from its usual sober obedience to law and order. His friend responded: "Look again, and tell me who is smoking." And my American friend was astonished to find that there was never a smoke in the elevator. Everybody held his pipe quietly in his mouth. Every man effectively obeyed the law in the quietest possible manner, kept his pipe in his mouth, but emitted no smoke in the elevator; and the same was true at the Underground station where people pass from train to stairway or elevator. The law was obeyed in the spirit in good faith.

On both sides of the ocean, and among all

ENGLAND'S PROTECTION POLICY

the allies, it should be well understood that England is fighting a tremendous battle, not only for English civilization, but for the maintenance of her Empire, and to the limit of her power she must not permit disintegrating forces in her trade and credit relations.

And, we Yankees should remember that any assaults upon the trade of our allies would be now, "in bad form."

We are building ships to help the world and to bring down freight rates that are tenfold too high and not to intercept, or interrupt, the trade lines of our allies.

We must give our European friends full time to get the billions that they have put into the battle for freedom back to the home base.

By the same rule under which we should not allow Germany with stolen machinery to jump into a trade contest with Belgium and northern France, we should not use the strong financial position which the United States has attained in the war as a leverage against the trade of our allies.

I asked an English banker and expert in exchange what I might expect if I appeared at the Bank of England with some five-pound notes and asked for gold. He replied: "You would probably get the gold, for the Bank has not yet refused it. But your name and address would be taken and it would be perfectly proper to inquire the purpose for which you desired the exchange. Your business, your record and your action would be inquired into to determine if you were really a friendly ally. And you might have less trouble than most people are having in England to get passage out of the country. Probably no attention would be paid to a few freak gold pieces, such as those with which you surprised, on your trip last year, the children here who were not old enough to remember the time when gold was current coin, and paper one-pound notes and paper ten shilling pieces had not been invented; but the export of a single gold piece is treason under the existing war laws.''

IX

Protection and Protected Shipping

LONDON, *March, 1910.*

WHILE the United States is swinging away from protective policies—from protective tariffs, from protection of its citizens abroad from protection to trade and citizenship—Great Britain is broadening her protective policies and will shortly show the fruit of some things she learned from America and which America is now forgetting.

England's protection began in defence of her citizens around the world on land and sea. Then she protected accumulations, thrift, savings, property and wealth.

In this war she saw clearly through to the end, and knew she could win the war only if she were well buttressed in finance. Therefore, the government guaranteed finance from the beginning, put the Bank of England and the British Treasury behind not only the circulating medium, but behind all the bank credits and the £350,000,000 of international bill credits. There is still in government storage about £15,000,000 uncollected of these pre-war financial bills.

While she has protected her citizens and their accumulations around the world, she has never protected trade prices or the individual as a laborer or producer. England has boasted her individual freedom; every man in the Kingdom was free to become the head of the government as prime minister or drop to the gutter in disease and death.

The English working man was free from Saturday to Monday to guzzle himself in beer, lower the physical and the family standard, and then on the days he chose to work attempt to compete in free markets with the free labor of the whole world. He was the glorious free Briton—free for Heaven or Hell in any way he chose.

The English merchant, manufacturer or producer had to compete with the lowest paid labor of the world. He was up against the machinery of America and the organization of Germany, and the government would give him nothing beyond blue book statistics and information.

PROTECTION AND PROTECTED SHIPPING

England now faces three problems of protection. She must protect or perish.

She must house her working classes under better conditions of sanitation and social association. She must insure the supply of raw materials for her industries. She must protect and regulate shipping and rail rates as related to English industries. Later she will go as far as necessary in extension of protective policies.

The United States today has little comprehension of the strained situation in England or Europe. England is at war until the peace pact is signed. Trade, transportation, food, rents, housing, coal and many other things are all under control. The trade of the Empire is subject to orders-in-council. Export and import is regulated first to protect finance, the gold of the Empire, next to protect the trade of the Empire and soon it will be regulated to protect the people from unemployment.

England will be many years in reconstruction and it is just as necessary that there be government control and trade regulations in after war reconstruction as during the war.

In every protection policy of Britain, ships are fundamental. As previously stated,

A WORLD REMAKING

Britain had half the mercantile tonnage of the world before the war, and for ten years had averaged to build 61% of the world's new shipping; and into ships went one-third of her coal production, three-quarters of it for exports, balancing imports of food, and raw materials. Startling is the record, in view of the English coal situation today, that three-quarters of the weight by cargo in English ships was coal.

Broad students of the oil situation have lamented the narrow consumption base of fuel oil. The wide fluctuations in oil have given rise to much scandal, and possibly to government prosecution of the Standard Oil which has persisted in a "bear" position in oil production as it was a buyer of oil, and its refiner, manufacturer, and merchant distributor in many hundred forms. It drilled for oil only to stimulate production and lower the price.

The opening of a new field, the bringing in of a gusher, any falling off in business were for many years sharply reflected in the market. Oil was without stability in production or consumption.

The simple mind and early training of John D. Rockefeller taught him to avoid the pitfalls of mining gambles, but to hold the strong-

PROTECTION AND PROTECTED SHIPPING

est faith in the ultimate consumption of all the oil produced. Rockefeller always testified to the hazard in the oil business and the outside world always laughed and attributed sinister motives to the testimony. Yet his testimony was true.

Only a few years ago experts viewed the danger to the oil market from the Mexican oil gushers and it can be well argued that disorder in Mexico—85 governments in 97 years, it is said—retarding her oil development has been a world blessing in disguise.

Steadily from Texas and Mexico oil has crept up the Atlantic coast, displacing coal and steadily oil from California has worked down the west coast of South America. But the great open field for competition of fuel oil with coal has been with respect to shipping. Here the difficulty has always been in the absence of fuel oil distributed throughout the ports of the world from which ships have to be bunkered. With coal in all ports and oil in only a few, oil for fuel was not attractive to shipping men.

Nevertheless the possibilities of driving coal burning ships from the ocean with steady supplies of oil in all ports has long been foreseen. Before the war, Germany was bidding

A WORLD REMAKING

for an oil base in Mexico. Canadian railroad interests were looking for the same thing and the Cunard Steamship Co. had vast plans for obtaining from Mexico a supply of fuel oil for its ships in every port of the world. These negotiations have now been resumed in London since the armistice.

But more important than any individual oil or shipping contract is the determination of the British government to control oil supplies over the world in the interest of its shipping.

To this end it has come into control of the Persian oil fields and it is now working closely with Royal Dutch and Shell interests and vast oil interests in Mexico to put a fuel oil base under English ships and commerce.

This is the great after-war trade development in England.

This subject can not be disposed of by repetition of the report in the "City" that Cowdray has sold control of the Mexican Eagle Co. to the Royal Dutch and Shell oil interests for $60,000,000 or $75,000,000.

I know that big oil interests have been after Cowdray's holdings in Mexico for many years, but Cowdray is too loyal a Briton to pass such a scepter of power into alien hands.

PROTECTION AND PROTECTED SHIPPING

I can not confirm the detailed financial reports that are now in vogue on both sides of the water, but I can declare that negotiations are going on between the British government and the Mexican Eagle Co. and the Royal Dutch and Shell Oil and other oil interests that are of the most sweeping and revolutionary character.*

They affect the trade, the shipping and the defences of the whole world, and Washington is asleep—or worse.

An international committee with high-sounding banking names has just been announced as organized to look after European and American interests in Mexico. Negotiations for this were begun by the state department at Washington last year. England and France were invited to co-operate. The United States desired a 50% representation on the commission, but Great Britain and France responded that their interests in Mexico were $600,000,000 and those of the United States somewhat less.

Later Washington replied that interests of the United States were paramount geograph-

---
*Cowdray later sold control of the Mexican Eagle Oil Co. at £6 per share but told his friends to hold on and the shares later advanced to £10.

ically. Now that position has been allowed and the committee has been made up as the United States proposed.

But what can this committee, or the state department in Washington, or the government of the United States do about oil in Mexico or oil therefrom for navy and mercantile shipping if other nations are to possess the oil properties of Mexico?

American pioneers and American capital secured possession and made the greatest commercial development from the Mexican oil fields formerly known as the "bad lands." One man holds on in possession in his field, E. L. Doheny of Los Angeles; and Cowdray is no more loyal to Britain than Doheny is to the United States, but Cowdray is backed up by his government.

Doheny is in London, insulted by his government at Washington, publicly and privately, and welcomed with open arms by every shipping interest in Britain.

He does not believe that the Royal Dutch and Shell Oil interests have been buying Mexican Petroleum shares in the New York market, but I have information quite to the contrary. This time I must differ from Mr. Doheny. He believes control of oil in Mexico

PROTECTION AND PROTECTED SHIPPING

is secure and locked up in the Pan-American Petroleum Co. and that he holds the keys. He thinks he can locate all the Mexican Petroleum Co. shares except about 50,000 in brokers' hands.

Mr. Doheny may get a surprise some fine day and the United States may get a bigger surprise. It may find itself building a navy and a giant fleet of mercantile ships on a coal basis when coal on the ocean has become useless, or on an oil basis that is largely foreign-owned.

A number of people have already settled in their own minds that the British government is in control of the Royal Dutch and Shell interests by acquisition of German or alien interests taken over during the war.

I happen to know that this is not the fact. I am not in England to dig out from a faithful ally its government or trade secrets. How England will control in the oil fields of Mexico and elsewhere has not yet been publicly announced, but English control there is to be with government backing of that control. The distributing organization, the alliances, the international relations and the part of the Standard Oil interests in England's oil program may, or may not, be revealed.

A WORLD REMAKING

Cowdray and Doheny have settled their territorial disputes and joined hands in the disputed territory. Their friendship is being daily cemented. Doheny has by far the largest oil interests in Mexico, Cowdray is second. There is no third. Each of these interests is putting out about 20 million barrels of oil per annum. With new pipe lines and ships, they could together in a short time duplicate for a time the world's supplies of oil. But they are both working judiciously and instead of increasing their output as tankers are being returned to them from war service, they are expanding their trade to distant parts, conserving their resources, increasing their revenues.

Twelve shillings for coal and fifty shillings for oil was the relative value five years ago, according to statistics worked out by experts. One ton of oil equals a ton and a half of coal in heat units. Then there is the saving in cost of stoking, in cargo space, in regularity of power, etc.; so that when bunker coal was twenty-five shillings a ton,—it is now much higher—a shipping man could quite well afford to pay seventy-five shillings a ton for oil.

But the whole problem is now, as years ago, to get a regular supply of oil and to have it bunkered around the world.

PROTECTION AND PROTECTED SHIPPING

Britain is preparing to supplement or displace her world-around coal bunkers by world-around oil bunkers.

The negotiations are largely through the Royal Dutch and Shell Oil combination which is more a holding combination than an operating concern. In the acquisition of properties the Royal Dutch takes 60% interest and the Shell Oil a 40% interest.

How the government stands back of these interests can not now be stated. But the power of England is there, is firmly planted, and is determined to defend itself both at home and abroad. In the words of Bonar Law: "A self-respecting government can do no less."

England has made very careful studies of the German Diesel engines as shown in submarine construction and Lord Pirrie is now quietly building twelve Diesel engine ships after the Danish pattern which he controls and claims to be better than the German. Washington is not alive to the Mexican situation, the oil situation, the shipping situation, or the Diesel engine situation.

Washington was asked by American interests to get from Great Britain plans of the Diesel engine as shown in the latest captured

German submarine. The answer was a doubt as to the courtesy of such an international request. Perhaps it might have a bearing on the new Poland, our mandate over Armenia or the Irish question. Washington had no conception of the meaning of the Diesel engine or its relation in the future to oil supplies and oil burning ships.

I will add one thing more "from under the rose." If Mr. Wilson should open up the Irish question with Lloyd George, he would very quickly learn something about the Mexican oil situation of which, it is said, he has been kept in ignorance—under his own instructions.

X

Remaking England In Men and Machinery

LONDON, *March, 1919.*

IN the war England prepared to sink or swim, but never to yield. The old England has been economically sunk in the struggle. What form the new England will take or how it will swim, no man is now wise enough to predict.

Every great war eats up a considerable percentage of accumulated capital and a large section of the capitalist class. But the energies of war create new wealth, new brain directors of wealth, and start a new capitalist class. If you doubt this, step into the theater in Paris, London or New York, and you will see that the old faces representing leadership in class, wealth and position have been largely supplemented by new faces bearing the stamp of labor rather than of leisure. The changed social condition is reflected everywhere—in art, entertainment, literature and social

A WORLD REMAKING

forms. The old must give way; the new creation comes in.

Never were prices of both necessities and luxuries so high. Never was the demand so great. Never was the circulating medium so abundant—with those who labor.

From the first outpouring of the national treasuries into the pockets of labor for war's defence come interesting stories concerning expansion in lines of luxuries, where luxury had never prevailed before. An English lady was carefully inspecting some furs and as usual with English ladies inquired the price. She admired a beautiful fur cloak and finally rejected it, saying, "Sorry, but I can't afford it."

The wife of a munitions maker from the Midlands immediately stepped forward and said: "I'll take that." Then turning toward the would-be-customer she exclaimed with an indescribable air: "Us is you now."

And so it goes over the world. The Red Guard in Russia says to generals, commanders and rulers: "Us is you now." The Southern cotton planter, white and black, says it to the North: "Us is you now." The western wheat farmer says it to Wall Street. Crowded theaters, dance-halls and

REMAKING ENGLAND

Jazz bands repeat the same refrain: "Us is you now."

But the whole world is living on its capital and dancing away in the aftermath of war its credit and its thrift, and no man may now say when the mad circle of debt, taxation and capital consumption will be run. The faithful recorder may only note the times and the signs, set down the facts and the figures and leave the wise and prudent to do their own guessing.

England is running a gamut of debt and taxation and labor payments from the National Treasury that means ultimate disaster unless she quickly and solidly rebuilds her entire industrial structure in man, machinery and transportation.

She is beginning with the essential machine—man. She is considering how to shorten his hours of work, strengthen him physically and mentally and increase his output.

She has forbidden the raising of house rents upon her laboring classes during the war; yet increases rates and taxes. The result is that the government must build not only 300,000 homes as planned a few years ago, but must financially assist in the construction of a

A WORLD REMAKING

million homes unless her people are to be encouraged to emigrate.

A million houses at an estimated cost of £600 each mean a national construction program that measures in money, very nearly to England's pre-war national debt which was just under three-and-one-half billion dollars.

I asked Lovat Fraser, the English economic and leader writer for the Northcliffe press, if my calculation was correct, and he said he could not dispute it. He added, however, that such a program could not be carried out except over a number of years. He said the first 300,000 homes, which were now being figured upon to cost nearly a billion dollars would require six billion brick, and the annual brick-making capacity in Great Britain was now only four billion.

I learned from other sources, however, that England is encouraging tremendous imports of lumber and has signed up contracts, of which the public hears nothing, for timber from around the world,—Scandinavia, British Columbia, etc. She is reaching out for timber as she is reaching out for oil and she will build and sail and defend as never before.

Lloyd George with his wonderful leadership has given her the keynote and it resounds in

REMAKING ENGLAND

all her constructive and upbuilding plans: "You can not maintain an A-1 empire with a C-3 population."

The housing construction program begins with an increase in the local tax rate of one penny in the pound. Then the national government advances money to the local government which, after construction, pays it back as best it can from the penny in the pound tax and the rents. But the return of the money is not so important as provision for sanitation and the safeguards against crowded tenement construction. The new law permits only eight to twelve homes per acre as compared with present construction of fifty.

England will not only house her working class in the improved sanitary and social conditions but will regulate rental payments. And so long as necessary in the war reconstruction period she will defend her people against hunger by import of food somewhat at the expense of the national treasury and by compensation to working people where there is enforced idleness by reason of war conditions.

She is well organized by committees dealing with unemployment and where munition workers could not be provided with new situ-

A WORLD REMAKING

ations she has allowed them for thirteen weeks, 29 shillings for men and 25 shillings per week for women at the expense of the national treasury. This is now being cut down but there is not the idleness in England one would suppose from the summary closing of the war work.

Many hands are employed in the substitution of peace machinery for war machinery and many orders and much work suspended by the war are still found available for competent hands. Of course, there will always be shirkers and those who desire to live upon the labor of others, but the banner carried in a recent workmen's parade read: "We want jobs, not doles."

Where war workers of the female sex refuse to go back to housework or previous situations, the treasury allowance is summarily cut off.

What England must next undertake is improved machinery, the speeding-up of plants and unlimited output per man.

One of the interesting illustrations of what she faces here may be found in the shoe business. In 1913, H. B. Endicott of Endicott, Johnson Co., the largest boot and shoe makers in the world, was in London and looked into the question of possible competition from English manufacturers. He understood full well the efficiency of United Shoe Machinery equipment then being offered from the United States to the whole world. Indeed, Mr. Endicott was not only the largest user of the United Shoe Machinery machines, but a director of the company. It would seem an easy problem for European hands to turn that machinery and with wages prevailing in Europe, be able to export shoes to the States. Sole leather and upper leather on both sides of the Atlantic ruled at about the same price. Mr. Endicott's final decision was that the United States had nothing to fear from the labor of Europe. Indeed Europe had most to fear from competition with the United States, for English wages had got to advance, he declared, and they might be advanced before the output and the efficiency increased.

I have never known a man of keener insight into business and financial problems than H. B. Endicott. England's position today is exactly what he foresaw and it would have been similar, although of slower realization, had there been no war. Wages have advanced and the problem now is to speed up machinery and efficiency to support the wages.

A WORLD REMAKING

Before the war, shoes were 25% cheaper here, but the United States could compete because it made better styles and fits. Today the situation is reversed and shoes are 25% higher in England than in the United States. If the shipping situation were normal, the United States would hold an advantage over Great Britain in manufacturing costs of shoes of $1 per pair.

A shoecutter formerly did 40 pairs per day in England for which he received a daily wage. In the United States he did one hundred pairs and there was no limit to his output or earnings. While the English shoecutter had an output of 40% of the American shoecutter, his wages had to be less than 40% because the factory and overhead charges per man were about the same in each case. This may be illustrated by recently compiled statistics showing the comparative cost per dozen pairs for actual labor and overhead. It was £2 10s 1d in England and in the United States £2 1s 6d, an advantage of 8s 7d per dozen for the United States. This equals 17 cents per pair advantage for just labor and factory cost of manufacture without leather or any other costs.

Labor costs per pair were about the same.

REMAKING ENGLAND

The 17 cents per pair advantage for the United States was fully accounted for by the increased capacity which lessens the overhead expense per pair. These are recently compiled statistics and are figured upon the war base for English labor which has advanced more than in the United States.

In the eastern district of the United States the cost of living and the cost of labor in the shoe districts have each advanced about 60%. Leather costs have advanced far more. Sole leather has gone up from 18 cents to 42 cents in the States and kids from 20 cents to 60 cents, with even greater advances in some other materials. The result is that of four different styles of women's shoes, comparative United States' costs in September, 1914, and September, 1918, show an advance in wages from 109% to 135%.

Nevertheless, shoes that now retail in the States for $8 and $9 are $12 shoes in England and on the Continent. The United States shoes for laborers that have advanced from $2.10 before the war to $4 and the women's shoes that have advanced from pre-war price of $1.60 to $3.20 and $3.60 are still well below European prices.

Manufacturers in New England could land

shoes in France at 35 francs per pair that retail in Paris at 60 francs and they could well afford to pay the 3 franc per pair duty for the higher grade shoe and not in the least fear the competition with English shoes that have to pay only 2 francs per pair duty. Low-priced shoes can not so readily compete for the French duty is without regard to price and quality.

While upon this subject of American shoes, it may as well be noted that American retail stores in France are now allowed to bring over 50% of their pre-war importations, but American importations to England are practically cut off by British government orders-in-council.

England is now under shipping protection, and she must rebuild and reconstruct quickly before a "free ocean" returns.

XI

Reducing Hours and Increasing Efficiency.

London, March, 1919.

ABOVE all countries in the world, England stands for conservatism. It takes a long time to arouse England to any necessity for change; when convinced she is thorough. It took her two years to understand the war in which she was engaged. It will take her three years to get well under way in the industrial reforms which must follow.

No other country surpasses England in production of leaders. The democracy of England promotes freedom of thought, expression and action. Yet the conservative English sentiment, translated into the American vernacular, is "I'm from Missouri and must be shown."

More than any other country, England is an open field and an open book. Before the war, the Germans were free to sail in and out of every port, bank in every city, build, borrow and lend, explore and map every corner of the island. The brain of the Jew was as welcome as the brain of the Gentile. Production from any race, any quarter of the globe, was welcomed. The Empire grew because it drew from all quarters—men and materials.

It will be many a year before Great Britain is again so open a book. Britain must now enter the field of intensive home human cultivation.

Lord Leverhulme has taken leadership in demand for what to most people would seem inconsistent—a six-hour day with increased production, greater efficiency and the lowering of prices to hold English exports in the markets of the world. He operates 93 factories and made England the greatest soap exporter in the world. Before the war, the exports of soap from England exceeded those of the United States, France and Germany combined.

Leverhulme has crossed the ocean 40 times; and travelled on nearly all the railroads of the world. He is the typical independent Englishman speaking his mind freely but frankly. When honors and title came his way, he yielded none of his independence. "Would

THE RESULT OF SHORTER HOURS

he kindly suggest a name for the new lordship?" He replied: "Leverhulme," his two family names. The officials protested and said it was without precedent. His simple response was it would be that or nothing; and Leverhulme it became.

Twenty-five years ago, he changed his working forces so far as possible from two 12-hour shifts in the day to three 8-hour shifts and the increased expense in production was inconsiderable.

A year ago he summoned his managers and asked them to figure on changing the 8-hour shifts to four 6-hour shifts.

The employees were called into conference and it was found that a domestic problem was involved. The housewives objected to a 6-hour night shift which might bring the head of the house home at four o'clock in the morning disturbing the wife and the school children. It was therefore arranged that, when the 6-hour shift was inaugurated, it should divide into three shifts of five hours and twenty minutes, and one night shift of eight hours so that a man worked one week on the night shift from 10 p. m. to 6 a. m. and during the other three weeks in the month completed his day's work in five hours and twenty minutes.

No workman could ask for more leisure for education, exercise, the enjoyment of family and social recreation, art and the open country.

The 6-hour day is not the simple proposition of just reducing the day's work from eight hours to six. It is a financial and industrial problem, and possibly experiment, of keeping down the machinery and overhead expense per unit by speeding up machinery, making an unlimited output and by intensive work both of man and machinery producing a larger output per hour and therefore at reduced cost. The machinery and the overhead can be run and can produce for 24 hours, but the man behind the machine must have a shortened day of labor in order to have an increased per hour output.

Although Lord Leverhulme has written a book upon the 6-hour day, I was most interested to hear him expound his plan before working men. I went with him to a Sunday evening meeting of railroad employees where he spoke for an hour and answered all their questions for half an hour.

Leverhulme is over 70 years of age, but

THE RESULT OF SHORTER HOURS

most energetic and instructive. He put forth the principles which underlie England's international trade with a clearness that I had never seen equalled by any public speaker or writer; business man or professor.

He declared that there was no affair in life that was in itself a simple proposition. Every movement, as well as every reform, interlocked other movements and reforms. One must be careful in changing an economic, social or trade basis that no mistake be made. A mistake might be a disaster to England. He had laid his plans for a 6-hour day in his factories a year ago. While their execution had been delayed when the war cut down his supply of raw materials by 40%, the 6-hour day would soon go into his factories for an attempted solution of the problem of improved social conditions, and shorter hours for working men.

Leverhulme was emphatic that improved conditions and increased wages must be united with increased output and reduced prices that consumption might be increased. To maintain consumption, articles should be abundant and cheap, and as 95% of the workers were the consumers, advancement of labor was based upon the complete circle of large production and large consumption.

This spelled low prices for goods and it could be made to spell high prices for efficient production. This was the gospel for high wages, low prices and exports.

He declared England could survive only by increasing output and efficiency and reducing costs, and that not the least part of increased efficiency would be the improved condition of labor.

When Leverhulme's engineers sent their automatic coal handling machinery to Japan, it was never set up. It could not in operation compete with labor in the Orient at ten cents per day. He had seen Japanese women carrying babies on their backs, and 40 pounds of coal on their heads and thus loading ships at 5d per day. What was the purchasing power of such labor and such wages!

"We must have unlimited output and exports," he exclaimed. "Increased wages make increased purchases and bigger production. There is not a man or woman in this hall that has not some unsatisfied want. If there is let him raise the hand. You can't produce too much if you will produce it cheap."

THE RESULT OF SHORTER HOURS

In the brief address I was invited to make following Lord Leverhulme, I probably received more instruction than the audience.

It is not altogether by asking questions one may sound out positions. It is sometimes by doing the talking and measuring the interest of the auditor. The glories of national defense, the sacrifices at the front, and the victory for the Allies did not appear a live issue in that hall, although "the hope of the world in an alliance of the English-speaking nations" was loudly applauded. When I told them that they had got to do their own thinking, I found that I had struck the heart of the situation. When I told them they were not working for themselves but for their children and their children's children, I knew I was on the right track with that audience. When I declared that education was their only safety, the applause was all that could be desired.

Later from many sources, I got the same keynotes. It was not increased wages so much as improved social conditions that labor was demanding. Lord Shaughnessy, of the Canadian Pacific, told me a few days later that if people would stop talking about labor problems and go among laboring men, there would be fewer problems to settle. Herbert N. Casson, the efficiency expert, said that his panacea for labor troubles, always a sure cure, was to have the managers, the directors and the owners all go through the same gate with the working men.

It was the working men themselves who started the Workers' Educational Association which began ten years ago in Lancashire, and to this Sir Ernest Cassel has given an endowment of a half million pounds.

I am convinced that English labor organizations are fighting their battle upon a far higher plane than the American labor organizations.

In the United States there is a large foreign element, migratory, uneducated and ever ready to listen to any form of political claptrap that will put something into their pocket from the pocket of another. But the English workingman is demanding education and social and industrial advancement more for his trade, his family and his children than for himself.

The greatest demand for education today is in England. Even the taxpayer is beginning to figure on the cost of waste in public education, for it is estimated that here it

THE RESULT OF SHORTER HOURS

costs at least a hundred pounds of taxpayers' money to give public school education to a child. Then a large part of that investment is lost because neither the child nor his education is properly protected.

The great deficiency in education, the world around, today is on the subject of capital appropriation and destruction by taxation. Here again England has begun to awaken, and people close to the government tell me that they shall soon recommend that England bid for the capital of the world by removing from foreign capital the taxation restrictions.

Now there can be no free movement either of gold or of capital. The movement of gold is interdicted; the movement of capital is restricted by burdensome double taxation.

England may be first to see the danger and make foreign capital in England free of tax. There may be a wrench in the economic situation of the United States if both capital and labor migrate from it at the same time after the conclusion of peace.

But English taxation may set up a counter current in forcing by taxation the home capital out of the country. England's lords of lands have been defeated in the financial battle against taxes; estates must be broken up. I have the highest authority for the statement that the English income tax today averages between eight and nine shillings in the pound, or between 40% and 45%. Notwithstanding that the income tax liability has been lowered to £130, or $650 income, only 2,200,000 people are found liable. Laborers and munitions workers now escape as farmers formerly did. But the war prices have made it worth while for the English income tax collector to insist upon farmers' returns.

It is fortunate that as Englishmen are forced to part with their estates under taxation pressure, there is a tenantry now getting good wages that is bidding good prices for land. A banker friend of mine asked an Englishman with whom he was spending the week-end, what his friend would do with the money coming in from sale of his landed estates. The reply was: "I don't know yet, but I am seriously considering getting my money together and taking what I can gather up to America where I may take out citizenship papers. I can not live much longer on the small income that is left to me after government taxes."

Every large estate in Great Britain recog-

THE RESULT OF SHORTER HOURS

nizes that today taxes and death dues have a lien on three-quarters of the income. Many a lord has complained in Parliament that he had only 2s 6d left in the pound of income, and one trustee told me that the landed estate in his charge left only one shilling in the pound for the beneficiary, for the tenants demanded improvements and expenditures which the tax authorities would not allow as expense.

XII

THE SPIRIT UNDER BRITISH FINANCE AND BUSINESS.

LONDON, *March, 1919.*

WHILE Great Britain fronts the greatest problems that have ever faced an empire, she is breasting them with faith and resolution truly sublime. The keynote for the United States should be "Look and Listen." The solutions of the European problems should have much in them of value for financial and business America.

The spirit that is under the business of the empire is well shown in the words that come to me from a midnight conference of bankers who had recently to go over the international exchange map and study the effects that might follow in British trade from two important events: the withdrawal of government support from international exchange and the declaration of peace at Paris.

This was the financial sentiment: "We

BRITISH SPIRIT IN COMMERCE

were prepared to fight to the bitter end; five years more of warfare did not affright us. Now is it not just as necessary to support the country in peace and trade reconstruction as in war's destruction? Europe is poor; she would have been poorer had the war continued. Should we not grant credits just as freely in world rebuilding as in world destroying? We are trustees in this war for all we hold, and the war is not over until the world and our empire of trade are reconstructed.

"The banks must continue to stand behind the government and the government behind the banks. The merchants must support the government and the government must support the merchants. The bankers must grant credits to both and regard themselves still as trustees and the country the first beneficiary to be considered.

"We have choice between permitting the ruin of nations or unlocking the whole economic situation of the world. Credits must be more liberal than ever before. Loans must be renewed as never before and time repayments must be extended as never before.

"Distant peoples must have boots and shoes; clothing and food; tools and machinery; and we must not now expect payment from the first crop for seeds, or tools."

England is now rapidly preparing to build the Dover tunnel, that long-talked of connection under the English channel between France and England. It will be built in much quicker time and at much less cost than is popularly imagined.

If I were to hazard a guess, I should say that Lord Cowdray's engineering firm would build it, because Cowdray and his organization are of the size to fit the job.

There is one thing about a sound engineering mind: while highly imaginative, it never dodges the facts. Cowdry said to me frankly:

"Financial and commercial affairs were never worse than today. They will straighten out in time or as soon as people understand the truth. The world will not long remain in its present condition of madness.

"In England, the working classes were never before so well fed, and England and her workmen will never go back to the conditions prevailing before the war.

"Never before have millions of people in Great Britain known what it was to have good food in unlimited quantities. Wages have been increased 100% and they may go back half way, but not lower. Therefore we may never expect to see again the pre-war prices of 50 shillings for pig iron and five pounds per ton for steel.

"Double shifts in many industries can pay 50% increased wages and get it back out of reduced charges on capital. We must have piece work and unrestricted output.

"There is no finer workman in the world than the British workman, if you are absolutely straight and fair with him and treat him as a human being. I have never found him to fail. The British workman is a sportsman and knows what is fair play. It is only when you hit him foully he begins to retaliate.

"I am not afraid of reduced hours for labor. Efficiency is not in long hours.

"In railway construction and other contract work, we have found that seven hours a day is the limit for piece work, with men stripped to the skin. They are never expected to work more than seven hours. That is the limit in physical efficiency."

Nowhere in the world is the copper situation encouraging, for the metal producers. The war has left the allies with more than 600,000,000 pounds of copper. This with the accumulations of producers makes a surplus in the world's supply of nearly one year's peace demands.

Before the war, the world's production had not varied for some years 10% from 2,000,000,000 pounds per annum.

The stimulus of war and the incoming of mines in Alaska and South America increased the production by nearly 50% and far beyond the peace demand.

Copper is one of the most necessary things in war, as is shown by the fact that it is regarded internationally as one of the most highly contraband articles of war. Had our government not restricted the price, copper would have sold at 40 and 50 cents per pound.

The sudden ending of the war, the stoppage of munitions, the failure of development in transportation under government control and the inability of the mines to curtail their output promptly, yet with safety to the organization, have all been factors in mounting up the copper surplus. Mines are deeper, organizations more expensive and what to do to avoid temporary disaster in copper mining production is a serious problem.

And there are possibilities right ahead of still further increased production from low-cost mines in Alaska, South America and Africa.

Ten years ago, Tanganyika in Africa was talked of for copper possibilities. Then for some years it was almost forgotten internationally. During the war, it has come forward to a producing basis of 60,000,000 pounds per annum. It is good opinion in London that the output of this district will grow up to 200,000,000 pounds and at a cost not exceeding ten cents per pound.

Almost nothing has been sold in the copper line since the armistice and there is no trade today in the world that needs more close attention and possibly government assistance in curtailment than that of copper mining.

The world in the future needs all the copper that can be produced, but meanwhile machinery and organization and ground openings must be maintained.

I have heard of only one sensible suggestion for the protection and preservation of the copper industry and that is from Sir Charles Henry, who next month will be in the United States.

He has been for years the London representative of American copper interests. When

A WORLD REMAKING

I asked him what the outlook was, he replied:

"I can see only one solution for copper. The companies should all come together with their surplus stock, join it with the surplus stocks of the allied governments, and put the whole in warehouse to be locked up for a series of years, or until the world needs it.

"The collateral is good and bonds should be issued against this copper, redeemable as the copper is sold some years hence.

"Then the mines should be allowed to combine and produce only so much copper as the industry will absorb. This will sustain price which will enable the mines to keep their organization pending industrial reconstruction."

Unless some such plan as Sir Charles suggests is inaugurated, I can foresee very bad times and unnecessary world waste in the copper mining industry.

There are 707 members in the new House of Parliament and seats for only 400. Never were there so many business men. Never were there so many new faces and never was there such a demand for information. It would seem that the standing members were

BRITISH SPIRIT IN COMMERCE

just as busy as the seated members in asking questions.

At present members are limited to eight questions a day. Recently I noted 116 questions in the Parliamentary Record and the next day 202 questions to be answered verbally and 48 calling for written answers, a total of 250.

If there were more enterprise in the English press, or ever American newspaper correspondence, a vast amount of useful information might be dug out of these Parliamentary replies. But what can be expected of a press fighting for its existence against a government still controlling the supply of paper material.

The London Statist has had to pay as high as a shilling a pound for its paper although the price is now down to 12 cents per pound.

New York newspapers cried "ruin" when newsprint advanced from under three cents to six cents per pound, but the dailies in London had to pay 12 and 14 cents per pound. Nearly all the daily papers still present a poverty appearance, and are badly printed on bad paper. The London *Times* is still in good form.

Although Northcliffe remains long in the

south of France, I am informed it is not true that any of his 53 publications are for sale. He resigned as chairman of the *Daily Mail* to be relieved of detail. He was warned by his physician many months ago that he had overworked. He believes now that his only trouble is bronchial. The Lloyd George party would not object to its permanency. They fear Northcliffe is only in retreat to pile up ammunition.

This Cyrano of the English press is twirling his rapier in air and now and then delicately touching a spot in the armor of Lloyd George.

But Northcliffe is not to have it all his own way if money can fight on the other side. Financial and journalistic forces have lined up behind the Prime Minister and Bonar Law is making good in leadership. Lloyd George is not now troubled by advice either from Northcliffe or Beaverbrook. The latter is also seeking health rather than political restoration.

Bonar Law's friends say he has never yet tackled a job he could not handle and that the loss of his two sons in the war has only nerved his arm for the Empire and the ultimate triumph of national and international law and order.

XIII.

Yankee Enterprise in Britain.

London, March, 1919.

CALLING men by their qualities rather than nationalities, I am willing to declare there are three Yanks in London from whom their cousins in the States can learn much. Two of them are most distinctly British by birth and would resent any classification outside of "British subjects." But they are all Yanks in enterprise and business daring. They are leaders in the English speaking world in banking, manufacturing and merchandising, and they get their business inspiration not only from the United States, but from world-wide observation.

They are Holden, Leverhulme and Selfridge and at times they drift as naturally together as chips on a pond. Selfridge addresses a London audience on the public service, the individual usefulness and the glories of the department store, not alone in London, but

A WORLD REMAKING

around the world, and Leverhulme presides and later asks Selfridge to teach him how to sell fish.

Rather singular you say for one of the leading manufacturers and exporters of England to have ambitions as a fishmonger, but have you ever noticed that when a man becomes a seeker or preacher of truth, how naturally he says: "I go a-fishing?"

When it comes right down to existence and subsistence, England stands upon ships, coal and fish.

The British Isles are on the lines of great fishing beds, but neither the production nor the distribution of fish has ever been systematically or scientifically developed.

Next to Great Britain and Ireland, the biggest island in the British Isles is Lewis Island on the west coast of Scotland. It has 777 square miles, 30,000 population and possibilities of great fishing development. Lord Leverhulme has bought it and has ambitions to make it a great center of British fish production, sustaining a population of 300,000 people. This will require not only considerable expenditure of capital locally for railroads, warehouse construction, etc., but some changes in the crofter laws and a vast business organization with retail fish stores throughout England.

If you want anything done, and well done, always go to the busy man. It is the men that have done that may do. Only a man like Leverhulme, who deals with laws, labor problems, national and international production and trade could undertake such a vast and possibly revolutionary project.

But Leverhulme's interests belt the world and it is perfectly natural that he should seek the ocean's depths for the play of his business genius, while he seeks business development in the skies; for he is already figuring how he can use aeroplanes and aeroplane forces to explore his forests in Africa and map out the rubber and cocoanut districts.

No wonder Leverhulme should say to Selfridge: "Teach me quickly the points of retail organization," for Selfridge knows merchandising to the individual wants of the consumer as does nobody else in the world.

He has his great London block of stores now so well organized that he complains he has nothing to do. He fears indolence and idleness and is just itching for the return of peace conditions when he may build something bigger than he already has in expansion of his present stores, which have not only spread out the whole length of the block, but have crossed Oxford Street and begun expansion on the other side.

Meanwhile Selfridge lectures on architecture and its development as represented in the department store, studies the history of trade from the time of the Phoenicians and publishes a big volume thereon, sees that all of his employees who went to the front get their wages and are advanced just as though they had stayed at home, and he takes the greatest delight in finding that the laws and principles of service which he has endeavored to unfold in his work are taking root in the minds and hearts of his staff and employees.

When I wrote of his store last year and noted the trained voices of the modest, uniformed and well-mannered elevator girls, that article somehow got back to London and was passed around in the store. Later the proudly delighted elevator girls went to Mr. Selfridge and said: "We don't want the bonus. We want to do this for the love of the service."

Probably nothing in the career of Henry Gordon Selfridge ever delighted him more than this fruitage and lesson from his teaching and examples in the dignity and pleasure of service.

I might write more than one interesting column of the world's foremost banker, Sir Edward H. Holden, but it might serve only to increase the envy which is rising in the banking world over the growth of the London Joint City & Midland with its $1,600,000,000 of deposits and 1,300 English branches.

Holden's life is banking. He eats, drinks, sleeps, works and thinks banking.

When the pedagogue told the elder Rothschild: "I hope your son will know something besides banking," Rothschild quickly replied: "I hope he will know nothing but banking and then the house, the family and the fortune will be in safe keeping."

Holden's recreation formerly was to spend his week-ends selecting locations throughout England for new branch banks and in finding new branch managers. Now his week-end recreation or "afternoon off" is just a little shooting excursion all by himself when he "drops" a bank or two off the limb of the "City" tree, and London awakens next morning to find a Holden amalgamation by which some conservative old banking institution has been hitched to the star of the Midlands.

A WORLD REMAKING

I asked Holden some details concerning what he was doing and how he did it, for we have talked frankly and freely on both sides of the Atlantic. He replied:

"I have been engaged in bank amalgamation since 1888. In this latest amalgamation with the London Joint Stock Bank, I made the proposition one day; it was before the directors the next, and the whole affair was buttoned up in 48 hours thereafter. Another bank had been dickering over the matter for more than six months. Of course, I knew the assets and business of that bank full well before I made my offer.

"These banking amalgamations have prevented panics and failures and they have put credit under trade and the empire and I think the future of the British Empire in trade and finance will be greater than ever. But the future of the empire depends upon the position that the bankers take.

"There are two kinds of banking here. We lend on securities on three months' time in London and we make our profit by having the borrowers leave on deposit a measure of their borrowings.

"In the Midlands they do not want to leave their money on deposit and so they arrange with us to borrow by overdrafts, paying ⅛ commission as in other commercial banking.

"It is the safest kind of banking because it is based on character. Our branch manager knows where that man is, what he is doing all the time; whether he quarrels with his wife, or fails to attend church on Sunday. In London a man borrows on security and we don't know when we shall see him again.

"We have 1,300 branches and I can visualize every one of them. But no branch manager makes a loan above £100 without first referring it to us in London.

"We have 9,000 employees, including 5,000 women. Our men are beginning to return, but we shall probably keep the women until the end of the year and eventually retain 500 of those who have become specially competent.

"We have paid a war bonus, which should run off when living comes down, and of course wages have been also somewhat advanced. Advances throughout England have been more or less according to war's demand. In the textile fields the workers were increased only 30%, while in war work they were increased much more. Living expenses

A WORLD REMAKING

here on the island have been very high, but prices have got to come down in the future.

"We shall also find some shrinkage in our inventories, and bankers must always be prepared for losses when their customers' assets shrink.

"We have a capital of £7,000,000 and £7,000,000 reserve, but I intend to put them both up to £10,000,000 or in all $100,000,000. We paid 18% last year and earned three times that. Our stockholders clamored for more dividends, but I would not have it. We must expect losses and we must guarantee our business.

"Now we have a treasury currency, but we must be careful where we have a currency based on securities or non-liquid properties. The only proper banking currency is that which the goods liquidate.

"I don't agree with many of the banking principles upon which bankers all over the world are expanding their business. I believe in centralization and strength and then again in concentration.

"In my early life I first studied political economy, then logic and then for seven years law. My good wife helped me in my studies. I got out of the bank at 3 o'clock and caught the lectures at four, five and six and then got an hour's schooling at 8 p. m. I used to go to bed at 10 and get up at 5 and managed to put in a pretty good day's work.

"Now I leave the bank at 4.30, get two hours' sleep before dinner and after dinner my two reading secretaries bring me all the points that they have gathered for me during the day. My working secretary also comes to me and my four general managers sit at the table and we thrash things out.

"When I make an address, you can be sure that six men have gone over my statements to see that everything is accurate and so clear that any man in the street can understand it.

"I usually retire at 11, sleep until 8, and am in the bank again at 10 a. m. I am 70 years of age and am training McKenna (formerly Chancellor of the British Exchequer succeeding Lloyd George) and four vice-presidents so that the business of this bank will be looked after when I am gone.*

"The English banker has got to be generous in building back English export trade. This island depends upon its exports and it must get its cheap raw material, buy in the cheapest markets and sell at a profit.

*Sir Edward Holden died in August and was succeeded by Sir Reginald McKenna as planned.

A WORLD REMAKING

"If labor makes such rates as cut out the profit, the trade will fall down and labor will be out of employment and the matter will rectify itself."

One of the leading economists in England, discussing with me for many hours the international situation, says:

"I am not alarmed over our huge war debt. It was figured before the war that all the interest on consols came back into the investment market. Virtually the same thing may become true of most of the war debt.

"The gross income of Great Britain before the war, that is the income by wages, interest and profits, may be estimated at £2,400,000,000 out of which £400,000,000 was saved for reinvestment. Today the gross income on the same basis may be estimated at £5,000,000,000 and I estimate that, after taxes and the distribution of government interest, there will be a remainder of £600,000,000 for reinvestment per annum or 50% more than before the war.

"Nevertheless I look for riots and breadlines and troubles all around and at the same time I think I foresee rising prices and great speculations. All such happenings took place for five years following the Napoleonic wars.

"Russia is going through the stages of the

French Revolution and the land must be divided among the Russian people. But France and Italy must both be helped."

XIV

CROWDED PARIS AND OVERCROWDED EUROPE.

PARIS, *March, 1919.*

THE center of the world today is Paris. But it is not the Paris of old, with refinement in art, service and living. It is the Paris of turmoil, of peace problem struggles, of crowds, Bolshevik taxi drivers, American political headquarters and British political headquarters, with onlookers from all over the earth.

By official count I am privately told Paris has 800,000 more people today than were ever before within its walls.

But Paris is not alone in the European crush. People are so in danger of having to sleep on the sidewalk in London that strict inquiry is made in the vise of passports from Paris, how long you are to stay in London, if you are sure of your passage to America, etc. Many an important person summoned to Paris has found that his wife must remain in

OVERCROWDED EUROPE

London. Nobody can travel to Paris unless he has business there. It is good opinion that passport restrictions will continue for at least two years.

Shipping is restricted. War demand and the demand for homecoming troops bring tremendous pressure upon every available accommodation. The travel pressure continues all the way on to Egypt and Palestine.

While gasolene is abundant in London, it is still restricted in Paris and the streets are not crowded as are the sidewalks.

Taxicab drivers are for the most part grizzled pirates who have no polite "thank you"; only increasing demands.

The exquisite bouquet of French service is gone. It may come back when the stranger departs, Mars sheathes his sword and Theseus roams the world no more. The same is more or less true of London and other crowded European centers.

An English friend of mine the other day took a taxi at 2.30 p. m., called at a bank in the city and told the taxi man to wait. Taxi protested, demanded to be dismissed, said it was his time to eat and that the blankety-blank rich had no thought as to when the poor should have food.

"But," he added, "the revolution is coming and then you rich will get yours and all that is coming to you."

My astonished English friend stood his ground. Insults never move an Englishman. He said: "I took you at 2.30 and I will not dismiss you." After the cabman had made a scene at the bank and had been put out, my friend drove with him back to the West End and paying his fare, tendered a "pourboire" which the Bolshevik taxi man rejected and resented with more oaths and more assertions of his independence and contempt for the rich.

I said: "Why didn't you report him to police headquarters and his license would not have been renewed."

He replied: "What can you do now when service is so short and the demand so great? Service is absolutely out of hand and beyond regulation."

Another friend summoned by the United States government to Paris and the Peace Conference found himself obliged to go from the Hotel Crillon across the Seine to the Quai d'Orsay for official conference—not ten minutes' walk. It began to rain and he called a taxi. The driver demanded 15 francs or $3.00

extra to drive him over the bridge. My friend says: "I might have paid it personally, but as I was on an official visit, I could not charge Uncle Sam that 15 francs extra to cross the Seine and I walked in the rain. The result was that I spent several days in bed fighting pneumonia."

You have to bargain in both London and Paris for your taxi, say where you are going and often bribe; otherwise taxi may not have gasolene enough to complete your journey and when it comes to disputing with a taxicab driver as to the amount of his gasolene, he holds the advantage.

Several parties in Paris have had to break up at an early hour because the chauffeurs and taxi drivers demanded it. They said it was time to leave; the party must finish.

At one gathering the host settled the controversy and prolonged the entertainment for his guests by inviting all the chauffeurs and taxi drivers to come in and finish up the champagne and pate de foie gras.

I inquired of the proprietor of the most fashionable hotel in Paris why he put that dancing party away off on the side and limited the hours of dancing. He replied: "The police have already notified us that any entertainment in Paris must be brief and quietly conducted, and not in public view, and that we have really had more dances than we ought to have had although we've only had about one a month. You see the police are watching the international situation very closely. Where the trouble has broken out, as in Berlin, dancing and feasting have preceded the rioting. Please do not forget that there are people in Paris who have not enough to eat."

XV

The Social Unrest.

Paris, *March, 1919.*

PARIS is betwixt many fires. There is the peace fire as well as the war fire, the social unrest, the food disorganization and the Bolshevik illumination in the distance.

On the war line France has, of course, been the great sufferer. The world has fought its battle on her soil and over her ruined cities, towns and industries.

The world little realizes that the France that accepted the gage of battle against the Hun was a nation of 39,000,000 people and is today a nation of only 36,000,000 people.

It is a rude shock to the returned man from the Front to find that he comes back to worse conditions economically than before the war when he had fought to make things better. He finds disorganization, idleness, high food prices, poverty and distress. Nobody has told him the truth that the country is poorer for the war; that the sacrifice must be continued.

Previous to the war he was "economically obedient." Now having carried a gun and faced dangers he is not to be trifled with by society or the police.

When homes have been lost, the restraining influence of the home is likewise lost. In the great devastated area of France there was not only the loss of cities, villages, industries and soil, but the loss of the family. Husbands, wives and children have been separated in the struggle. I am told that many will continue in independent existence. This is one of the most grievous of the French losses.

As in England and elsewhere the demand is that the Germans pay to the full. In the Peace Conference the French hold the advantage. Their local sentiment has effect internationally. When the finance minister brings in the budget the deputies demand that they first know how much Germany pays before they will proceed to assess the country.

Paris is placarded all over with posters: "Let Germany pay first." France has not taxed herself as have England and the United

THE SOCIAL UNREST

States. Her response is that she is too poor already.

The income tax of France was made 3% after the war opened, then 6% with exemptions and for 1917 which was paid last year, it ran up as high as 20%, but this was for incomes above 550,000 francs.

The French also understand better than the people of other countries the necessity for the maintenance of property and income and they realize the dangers from excessive taxation in the destruction of the lifeblood of business.

When Socialists in London and New York point to a French proposal to levy a direct war tax on the wealth of the country they should inquire the basis of the proposal. In the by-play of politics, it was found desirable to create a certain sentiment. A friend of mine said to the finance minister: "You can get the effect you want by proposing a levy on all capital."

It was sprung in the Chamber of Deputies and the effect was all that could be desired, but there was an unlooked for after-effect. The French press and people, high and low, rich and poor, rose up and demanded the head of the author of such an infamous pro-

A WORLD REMAKING

posal and it nearly cost Finance Minister Klotz his portfolio.

Clemenceau privately told his friends: "I appointed a Jew as minister of finance because finance is the one thing the Jews are supposed to understand, but Monsieur Klotz is the only Jew who understands nothing of finance."

Nevertheless the brief agitation for a capital tax caused a tumble in Stock Exchange securities and an advance in pearls and other jewels as more easily concealed and therefore less liable to tax depreciation.

The French are on edge. I have asked many people in and out of France the cause of French antipathy toward President Wilson and somewhat toward the United States. Scientists say that all Europe has been put more or less on edge by a deficiency in sugar and fats and that there is now, for the time, nothing normal either with nations or people.

A year ago, France was sick of the war, wanted peace and nothing so much as peace. She never dreamed of possessing the Saar coal fields and would have divided on Alsace-Lorraine.

Today France has Alsace-Lorraine, but has not men enough to administer the provinces;

THE SOCIAL UNREST

therefore the German officials are still in charge. She wants the Saar coal fields in order that Germany may not possess them. She wants her frontiers not only on the Rhine, but over the Rhine and she wants Germany strangled and yet made to pay for all there is in her.

Under these circumstances one must make due allowances for the sentiment of the French against Mr. Wilson, a sentiment so virulent at times that Wilson told Clemenceau if the French criticism did not cease he would propose the removal of the Peace Conference to a more neutral country. The original American plans were for the Peace Conference at Geneva. And of course Clemenceau saw the point of not permitting the French to overplay their local advantage.

Not long ago Le Cri de Paris came out at 5 a. m. with a cartoon that would have delighted the Republican leaders in the States, but the French government suppressed it within an hour. There has been a great exposure in Paris of the impositions practiced upon buyers in the field of art, and many fake Rodins have been brought to light. The world knows the famous Rodin in stone, "The Thinker," which presents the aboriginal man with giant arms folded and head bowed in primeval thought. Le Cri de Paris presented this man of stone as "Another Fake. Rodin, The Thinker" but the face was not the face of a Rodin. Spectacles and all it was the face of Wilson.

In the heights of seriousness the situation is made or unmade ofttimes by a laugh and the French in caricature and wit are stabbing at Wilson.

XVI

Peace "Without Victory."

Paris, *March, 1919.*

EVERYWHERE the word has gone forward that Wilson is not pro-ally; that his pacifist sentiments carry him beyond the Rhine.

Mr. Wilson's friends give him credit for saving six months of warfare. They fail to see that by this boast of stopping the war, they confess that he saved Germany.

Everywhere outside Hun and pacifist circles it is now declared that the armistice came too soon and the declaration is that without the knowledge of the allies Wilson was talking with Germany.

If he takes credit for an early armistice, he may also take credit for that policy which to some was and is most offensive "Peace without victory."

In the pourparlers the American representative made certain demands, and an objection

A WORLD REMAKING

being raised, he said: "Then I fear the possibilities are that the American army will be withdrawn and our conversations will cease."

Quick as a flash, Clemenceau replied: "Will your conversations with Germany also cease?"

"On that I can give you no assurance," said the American representative.

General Foch at this time had conference with his generals as to whether they could successfully continue the war, the American troops withdrawing. Foch believed that they could as of course the Germans were then demoralized and on the run, while the spirit of the English and French was at the highest.

One of the French statesmen said: "Mr. Wilson, why do you wish to negotiate a peace now with Germany?"

Mr. Wilson replied: "Because Germany has been defeated."

The French reply was: "Germany does not know she has been defeated and that is all that matters. Furthermore Germany believes she was not defeated."

The French people were very much put out that Mr. Wilson would not go to see the devastated areas of France. His whole atti-

PEACE "WITHOUT VICTORY"

tude was that of a peacemaker who did not wish to see the worst because he might share in the hatred of the Hun and thereby be less serviceable to the cause of peace.

France must cry poverty now to make her exhibit at the Peace Conference for damages and collections, especially when the whisper goes forth that Wilson is against any German indemnity or any American military support to collect an indemnity.

When the settlements are over, and the prospect for collection good, the criticism and caricature of Wilson and the United States may fade away. The spirit of independence, insolence and self-assertion may then be of the past and the fine old flavor of politeness, brotherhood and service may return. It is inherent in the French character and nationality. It is absent more or less now from Paris because France has been crowded out of Paris.

A few days ago I went into the Hotel Crillon, the American official headquarters, and enquired concerning the 72 motor cars in the American service and made use of the perfect American telephone equipment that radiates thence over Paris and France with American-manned switchboards and the perfection of

A WORLD REMAKING

American telephone service. There are 396 American telephone exchanges here, including a few in England. There are seven in Paris alone. One with a trained American telephone ear would know that no other than Col. John J. Carty, the electrical head of the American Telephone wires, had built that system in France and still had his gentle yet perfect touch upon it.

Then I passed into the Place de la Concorde now filled with cannon trophies taken from Germany, the captured guns stretching in a long line from the Tuileries down the Champs Elysees to the Arc de Triomphe. I was due in a few minutes at the lunch to Wickham Steed, the new editor of the London Times. It was to be at 80 Champs Elysees, the Palais du Fayel which the French government with the nobility and graciousness which characterizes the official class in France has so generously placed at the service of the visiting journalists. The spring rain descended and a cab I must have. I appealed to two French taxi drivers. They replied most politely that they were engaged. "Would Monsieur wait a minute?" In different directions they walked or ran and in a few minutes a taxi was at my service. Not

PEACE "WITHOUT VICTORY"

a single franc could I pay them. "Was Monsieur bound for the Palais du Fayel? An American journalist? It was a pleasure to serve him!"

The heart of France, the heart of Paris, is all right when you find it. It is largely buried today, but the heart, high and low, is true. I know what Clemenceau feels, and he is the great, grand, struggling, fighting tiger of France. He feels that we ended the war, but that the armistice was too soon. The gratitude of France must be withheld until it is clear that the sudden armistice does not deprive France of a permanent peace by a "peace without victory."

XVII

Not Writing But Making a Peace.

Paris, *March, 1919.*

I ASKED Monsieur Geraud who writes in the Echo de Paris under the nom-de-plume Pertimax for a clear statement of what the French people really wanted. He replied instantly:

"We want something more than a declared peace. You have not to write peace; you must make peace.

"What Wilson says is in every French book dealing with the philosophy of peace for 200 years and for 200 years France has suffered by holding to these very ideals which we have heard from Diderot down, and more particularly since 1789. We went to war in 1870 with an old musket to fight Germany. We then believed all those things that Wilson is now so grandly proclaiming.

"We want no more false steps. When we give up what we have in our alliance, we may find in three or four years that we have given up something substantial for the same old idea that has been talked for 200 years and find there is no change in the record—6,000 treaties of peace and 50 wars in every century.

"We have been crushed under the principles of Wilson and nearly lost our life in 1870 by sticking to those principles. We now want something more concrete.

"You can't put a formula of right as a bird in a cage and find it will live there forever."

I asked the same question of Lt.-Col. Philippe Bunau-Varilla who with his brother owns the Paris Matin with a daily circulation of over a million-and-a-quarter, next to the Petit Parisien the largest in Paris. As every American ought to understand, it is to his sole efforts that the United States today owes the Panama Canal and there is a story here that has never been fully told. I may give it out some day.

The Colonel thumped his wooden leg on the hardwood floor of his beautiful French villa near the Arc de Triomphe—he had left one leg at Verdun—and said:

"The League of Nations must be more than an expression of philanthropic aspirations.

A WORLD REMAKING

It must be such a league that if Germany starts to make guns at Essen, it will not only be told to stop, but it will be stopped within so many hours and if necessary stopped by force.

"A law without sheriffs to enforce it is no law."

There is a financial and economic side to this opposition toward Wilson and the American position.

The French are a thrifty nation of producers, caterers, shopkeepers and entertainers. No race is quicker to profiteer when once restraints are lifted. The American is educated to the one-price store. He is thrown by his government into khaki uniform and shipped overseas with no knowledge of the language or of the customs. He does not understand that in the Latin countries the man who asks you ten francs for an article will feel no insult or resentment if you offer him one; he sees only that you are ready with him to bargain. The American youth comes out of the trenches feeling that he has helped to fight the battle of France. Then he wishes he could kill that "frog" that demanded five and ten times the price for a room, a breakfast or a cup of coffee.

NOT WRITING BUT MAKING A PEACE

The Frenchman sees his compatriot fighting on the sacrificial soil of France for the protection of the English-speaking world and at day wages one-twentieth those of the American soldier—"the pig." He sees in khaki sons of American wealth throw coins upon the counter for articles and leave the change behind. He does not know but that every American soldier boy is a multi-millionaire. Hence misunderstanding and disruption, with no organized propaganda for the promotion of good fellowship and the cementing of international relationship in defence.

Across the Rhine there is propaganda, organization and ordered cultivation of fellowship and the healing of the wounds of war that trade may quickly follow. Every German lass smiles upon the American soldier boy and every German shopkeeper wants to know quickly how he can serve him. Hence the military orders from American headquarters to stop fraternization.

But the American boy continues to smile at Gretchen. She quickly understands the orders and that she must not speak. But she smiles back and slips a pitcher of hot chocolate through the doorway. Food is cheaper on the east bank of the Rhine than it is on

A WORLD REMAKING

the west bank and the Frenchman is the greater sufferer from high-priced food.

When French eggs go from two cents to 12 cents per egg, you will get no thanks from the hen or its proprietor. But American invaders will be frowned upon and will be charged with ruin of the French poor. I would like from the Far East a phonograph record of the sentiments of the inhabitants of Bagdad and from around the ruins of Babylon just beyond when the invasion of the English forces sent up the price of eggs from six cents a dozen to 6 pence each, an increase of 2,300%. My information as to egg prices is exact. But my Rhode Island reds will get the news before this is printed and still further Bolshevik my farm capital.

War doubles the price of sugar in the United States, causes disorganization and revolution in Cuba and cuts the price in half in Java, impoverishing the producers there. The war puts wheat in Australia under $1 a bushel and in the United States above $2.25 a bushel; yet such are the inequalities of sacrifice in war.

Germany has inflicted a ten billion dollar damage in the war area, most of it in France. It is all visible to the naked eye. But the

NOT WRITING BUT MAKING A PEACE

people of England have suffered a far greater damage and disorganization, yet invisible, from the war. France can capitalize her damage. She is the world's entertainer and war has given her a "moving" picture show—without motion—which after peace she can stage and invite the whole world for its view.

As soon as the food and transportation situation is normal, the world will wish to view Rheims, Chateau-Thierry, Belleau Wood, Amiens, Peronne, Arras, Vimy Ridge and the devastated battle plain of the Somme. The roads, highways and pictures are all there, except for the growing, waving weeds. Every man who can afford to travel during the next five years, has ambitions in that direction. No motion picture can compare with it and it will be the exclusive exhibit of France. It will be forgotten that Anglo-Saxon labor, pounds and dollars have repaired and maintained the highways. The English have built in the southeast from Salonika to their battle lines against the Bulgarians, a highway costing seven million pounds, or $35,000,000, but the world will never visit it or use it and I doubt if it will ever be maintained for anything of value.

XVIII

Helpless Russia.

Paris, *March, 1919.*

THE Russian influence in Paris so closely allied with the French finance is also strongly against Wilson. The Russians declare that he has encouraged Bolshevikism and disorder, has spoken over the heads of the governments and appealed to the people in a way to cause confusion and worse; that he has never denounced Bolshevikism or the plunderers and murderers who are now dominating Russia in a terrorism worse than history has previously recorded. They say that on the other hand he is desirous of meeting, parleying, negotiating and perhaps settling with the Bolsheviks.

I had several talks with the Grand Duke Alexander of Russia. He said:

"I am not a Grand Duke here. I am just a plain Russian asking for justice for my country. I have sought President Wilson,

HELPLESS RUSSIA

Secretary Lansing, Colonel House and others, but they will not see me.

"Russia does not exist at the Peace Conference, and this is justice! What is the use of talking of the rights of man when 180,000,000 people are denied any right and have no representation and no consideration at this conference? Never once has President Wilson repudiated the Bolsheviks. Never once has he spoken for Russia, except one day in September—one day, through Lansing, he sent a message to the Soviet Congress. It is but justice to say that nobody then knew what the Soviets were. Here is the ruin of Russia and its civilization.

"Six months ago it was said to be a question for Russia, but I declared it was a world danger and that the world should act in self-protection.

"It is no longer any question of Russia. My ruined country has become the center of Bolshevik propaganda. They have schools for the training of professional people to make propaganda all over the world. They now attack the civilization of the whole world, and how will you make your defence? By trying to compromise with them? Will you compromise with murderers?

A WORLD REMAKING

"Wilson has only words. What peace can the world have when there is no peace in Russia? What is the use of talking about the rights of man when one-eighth part of the whole world of a billion-and-a-half people is treated as a negligible quantity?

"If the allies had acted against Bolshevikism immediately after the armistice, there would have been no Bolshevikism in Germany. Now the allies have encouraged it. The allies must occupy Germany to get their money. Then they must throw down Bolshevikism, or they don't get it. The Bolsheviks have proclaimed the weakness of the Peace Conference. They went into Germany and proclaimed that they alone had moral courage.

"Russia is today much worse off than under Tartar dominion. The Tartars were men; the Bolsheviks are brutes.

"My two brothers and my two uncles were murdered because of the criminal decision made here against Russia at Paris. They were killed on the 29th, or one week after the criminal decision of the 22d.

"The Commissionnaire telephoned the wife of Grand Duke Paul: 'Tomorrow he will be set free.'

"What torture and cruelty combined with

brutality! The next day they took these four grand dukes in a camion from the prison and let them believe that they had liberty. My oldest brother, Nicholas, was so happy. He took the cat that had been his prison companion along with him out into the sunshine.

"They brought them to the old fortress, put them in a cell and bade them take off their clothes for a change; really because the Bolsheviks did not want to spoil the costumes; and these four naked men who had never done anybody any harm in the world were stood up against the wall and killed with revolver shots. Thus died my two brothers and two uncles, and this is the Twentieth Century!

"One hundred and fifty thousand Allied troops could deliver Russia. The dirty work —and killing is dirty work—would be done by the volunteer army of Russia, but what is wanted is an allied police force behind to keep order and prevent any back fire as the patriotic troops go forward.

"I know that the Bolsheviks have killed 30,000 Russian officers who fought for the allies against Germany and for liberty and freedom.

"Russia was the first in the war, in the

common defense against Germany, and she suffers the most. What is the use of talking about liberty and the rights of man when there is a Russia with no rights, no freedom, and no existence at this conference?

"Three months ago the Bolsheviks were printing 300,000,000 roubles a week; now 500,000,000 roubles. Before the war the dollar was two roubles; now it represents 15 roubles.

"There are now 46,000,000,000 printed roubles afloat. In the year 1818 the income was only 2,500,000,000 roubles and the deficit was 43,200,000,000 roubles.

"Everybody has been disarmed; every objector killed. There is no use talking about rescuing the world if you can't rescue Russia."

XIX

WORK, NOT FINANCE, THE SOLUTION.

PARIS, March, 1919.

TWO appeals come up before the Americans in Paris studying the problems of peace.

First: Will the United States stand in with the allies and enforce terms of peace, or simply lay down the rules for peace and then abandon the field?

Second: Will the United States allow joint obligations arising from the war and pool them against joint resources; in other words, will America assist in refunding the war debt on a joint and unified basis, pooling liabilities and assets?

I had to respond most frankly that in my judgment the United States would never guarantee the European war debt, or join in any such guarantee; that we had better build a navy or a Chinese wall around us; that a nation with 10% indebtedness would not join

A WORLD REMAKING

a partnership or make joint debts with nations indebted 50%.

Could the United States exist independently? My response was that it could be sufficient unto itself and exist in absolute independence; that it was the only nation on earth that could make progress on that line; that it needed really to buy nothing in Europe except art and pleasure; that the United States would fight before it would join in European indebtedness.

So far as people are looking to finance as the main solution of peace problems, they are destined to disappointment.

Finance solves nothing. It is only a bridge from seedtime to harvest, from one country to another, or from security to security. The solution of problems of war is in men and in labor and not in money. The loss to the world is from loss of labor. In a single crop year the difficulties of the present situation would be adjusted if there could be security in peace, and Germany and every man in the world put at work with the world's machinery to produce and distribute with efficiency.

Everybody has wants, and desires are limitless. The only solution of Bolshevism, war debts, peace and prosperity it to set

WORK, NOT FINANCE, THE SOLUTION

the world at work, each man supplying his wants, producing a surplus, and thereby helping to supply some of his neighbors' wants. One year's full turnover of work and the world would be set on the right track.

On both sides of the English Channel I have been told that Wilson has become somewhat frightened over Bolshevism and that that was the meaning of his demand for a League of Nations, or a big American navy; also that he is less of a Socialist than when he first came to Europe.

There are people in Europe who want to frighten the United States with Bolshevism. I had to admit that we had our own form of Bolshevism which was steadily transferring the accumulated labor of the past, as represented by capital, to the consuming labor of the present by taxation in the interest of high wages.

But that when we came to face the red flag and the torch, the East Side Jews in New York City could command no large body of Red Guards and would not be able to disarm all the rest of the country as had the Jews in Russia.

The trouble with the world today is enforced idleness. The government of Germany that is issuing millions of paper marks to pay idle labor has the advantage for the moment over the United States that is issuing interest-bearing bonds to pay double prices to labor.

Great Russia is so far in idleness that less than two-thirds of the land upon which she and the outside world formerly depended for food has been planted. Paper money issues for deficits and idleness.

Belgium has been demoralized by idleness. It was a close vote with the British Cabinet as to whether the Belgians should be allowed to work for the Germans for wages or whether the British should pay them for idleness.

The other day an American relief ship arrived with food and American forces had to unload the ship while 100 Belgian longshoremen stood idle on the quay.

An English committee has been considering the situation of Belgium and in lieu of the 4½ francs per day for idleness it was voted that people should now go to work and that wages should be 7 francs a day.

When this was communicated to the idlers in Belgium, the response was: "Are you joking? You can't be serious! You surely

WORK, NOT FINANCE, THE SOLUTION

don't mean to offer two franc and a half per day for work. We get 4½ francs for doing nothing and your 7-franc offer is just 2½ francs per day for work. We can't accept it.''

One in position to have the broadest and the closest outlook into every country in the world says:

"The Americans have no conception of the European conditions. The situation is perfectly hellish. Five million people in Belgium and two million people in France won't work. They prefer idleness. Germany pays idle men more than they can get working and here is the Chicago Tribune yelling over the headlines of its Paris edition: 'Send back the American boys toute-de-suite.' This demoralization of military forces in Europe is one of the reasons we cannot go into Russia.

"If we had not stopped fighting but had smashed the Germans right back over the Rhine and dictated peace on German soil, the situation with the troops would have been easier.''

There should be no international scramble for trade, and, if there is, the United States is likely to raise some bad feeling. There is a sentiment here that the war was a joint defense; that the United States comes in late, dictates the terms of peace, loans ten billion dollars to the allies and may be soon in position, in finance, shipping and exportable surplus, to compete most favorably in international markets.

While, in the open, Paris walls ring with placards: "Let Germany pay first," there is sometimes an undercurrent that says: "Why shouldn't the United States pay, or at least pay back a part of the war profits it made early in the war when Wilson was holding to neutrality of thought?" It is figured here that the United States made five billion dollars war profits.

The United States has enough to do in filling up empty shelves the next three years without engendering animosities by injudicious, and perhaps unfair, international trade squabbles or attempts to gain future strategic trade positions at the expense of European cripples.

Prosperity in the United States with high wages may be something of an international danger, especially when there is enforced idleness, starvation, Bolshevism and Hun propaganda in Europe.

XX

INDEMNITIES AND SIGNATURES.

HOMEWARD BOUND.

I LEFT Paris after securing the best information possible upon the two peace problems I consider most vital to finance:

First, what will be the sum of indemnities and reparation demanded by the Allies from Germany?

Second, will Germany refuse to sign up?

On the first problem I was told in March that beyond a specific sum to be paid at the beginning, no round amount for reparation or indemnity would be demanded of Germany. But certain principles would be laid down under which Germany would be expected to make good to the full of her financial ability to pay and exist as a nation.

The total sum was computed at two hundred billion francs or forty billion dollars, but it would not appear as such in the peace document. It would be somewhere about five

A WORLD REMAKING

billion dollars down and the balance under certain principles of reparation and indemnities—principles that would be permanent and stand as international law between nations in any future aggressions.

While the French and other European nations might desire to put Germany under control and tax for 50 to 100 years, American interests were desirous of having the whole matter cleaned up within 20 years.

Helfferich's book showing the great value of Germany in 1913 was reprinted for use at the Paris Peace Conference to show what Germany can pay. The great banker, statistician and later finance minister, boasted the wealth of Germany in 1913.

The figures of Helfferich rise up as Nemesis, for to them the financial experts point and ask: "How much shall we add to Germany's value for the machinery and other goods stolen from northern France and Belgium?"

The Germans stripped Belgium bare of everything. The material damage is estimated at from two to five billion dollars, but tuberculosis is rampant throughout the country brought on by undernourishment and lack of fats.

The material damage in Northern France

INDEMNITIES AND SIGNATURES

is estimated at from four to ten billion dollars.

Upon the question of how promptly Germany would sign up on the terms of peace, the views were various. The general impression was that Germany, after due protest, would sign anything she had to sign. How long she would keep the terms was a matter of conjecture. Everybody admitted that there had been no change in the spirit of the Hun.

Everywhere in Germany it was reckoned that Germany had made a mistake and would have to pay, but nowhere in Germany was there any consideration of the moral wrong or the moral issue.

The war was regarded in Germany as an unprofitable business venture. Since it had failed, the best possible terms of settlement must be made.

Intelligent observers who have crossed the Rhine and been through Germany were firm in their conviction that Germany would not again fight, at least during this generation. But everywhere in Germany was the determination to get back by trade the position that had been lost by the blunder of war.

There was a minority view that the Ger-

A WORLD REMAKING

mans might adopt the tactics of the French in 1871, refuse to sign the treaty and say to the allies: "Take the country, run it and collect if you can."

The temptation for the Germans to do this is greater now than it was to the French in 1871, for there is the menace of Bolshevism. For the allies to now take charge of Germany means primary. expense rather than primary collection and the settlement of not only the German issue, but the issue of German socialism, Spartacism and Russian Bolshevism.

In 1871 Bismarck first demanded of the French six billion francs and Belfort, but Jules Favre replied: "Take the country and administer it. Do what you like. I resign." Bismarck replied: "I am afraid these are the best terms we can give, but come to me a little later."

When Favre returned, Bismarck said: "I have conferred with the authorities and Berlin and I induced them to reduce the demand to five billion francs and not take Belfort." Favre instantly replied: "We accept."

The ablest international bankers declare that until 1922 the world belongs to the producer and the manufacturer, the workers who

INDEMNITIES AND SIGNATURES

will restock the world's vacant shelves, and the merchant and the banker who will forward the goods. After that the effect of taxation will be shown; the world will be poor and goods and labor will fall. It is now most necessary that we have international co-operation and mutual help in restocking the world. This is more important than rebuilding.

The wisest among the international bankers say there should be no international scramble for trade, but rather co-operation. As one banker expressed it:

"Trade must be wisely regulated between the allies with regard to exchanges, money, etc."

It was estimated for me that there were 250 foreign correspondents in Paris watching for news of the Peace Conference. If all of them were turned loose in Germany they would learn little of value unless they reached the finance fundamentals and aims of the empire, and learned more than the picturesque side of Hans and Gretchen, their welcome to the American troops, the dancing in Berlin and the idleness and rioting in the towns that hope soon to be manufacturing.

An international banker friend of mine

A WORLD REMAKING

from South America crossed the ocean and front lines to secretly meet the bankers he had known in years past and learn the actual economic condition of Germany and her aims for the future.

It was with some difficulty he found the people he wanted. They were generally well out of public view or camouflaged behind some collateral occupation. But the American banker found them and had his heart to heart talks as of old.

He later reported to me as follows: "We talked with the utmost frankness. There was not the slightest regret as to what had happened, only that the issue had turned out with unfavorable results for the Germans.

"They were not interested in discussing causes; admitted Germany had been defeated and that Germany expected to pay through two generations.

"They were all ready, they said, to manufacture and trade with the whole world, but they appeared to me to have no conception of the psychology that they are up against when people refuse to do business with them.

"They expect to do an enormous business through Holland under Dutch names,

INDEMNITIES AND SIGNATURES

"They hate the Belgians first and the English next, are rather sorry for the French and are terribly anxious to do business with the Americans whom they respect because they are strong and rich."

I asked one of the largest English merchants what proportion of his sales before the war was goods of German manufacture. He replied about 10% and this agrees with the trade statistics of the Empire showing about 10% of English imports as goods from Germany.

I asked him what proportion of German goods he expected to sell after the signing of peace. His reply was: "Not a pennyworth. Only the other day I was offered a large consignment of goods from Switzerland concerning which I had my suspicion. I asked the Board of Trade as to the business and standing of the Swiss firm behind the goods. And the response was that they were rated as Swiss cheesemongers. I of course declined the goods. It will be many months before I can afford to put German-made goods on my shelves.

"The singular thing about this situation is that the Germans have not the slightest conception of the psychology when it comes to the offering of their goods over the world after the declaration of peace."

XXI

SOCIALISM VERSUS DEMOCRACY.

HOMEWARD BOUND.

ONE of the ablest brains in the United States, and whose lines of information run beneath the Peace Conference as closely as those of any business man, spoke to me with amazing frankness concerning the international situation. I do not care to give his name because he is too close to political and business influences on both sides of the water to be quoted with a frankness that might endanger some of his interests and associations. He said:

"If you believe in democracy you cannot believe in socialism. Democracy means opportunity for all. Socialism is the poison that would destroy democracy. Socialism holds out the hope that a man can quit work and be better off.

"Bolshevism is the true fruit of socialism. If you will read the interesting testimony

A WORLD REMAKING

before the Senate committee given about the middle of January that showed up all these pacifists and peacemakers as German socialists and Bolsheviks, you will see that a majority of the college professors in the United States are teaching socialism and Bolshevism and that 52 college professors were on so-called peace committees in 1917.

"The worst Bolsheviks in the United States are not only college professors, of whom President Wilson was one, but capitalists and the wives of capitalists who are confusing improvement of the social order with the theories of socialism and know not what they are talking about.

"Many women joined the movement, and neither they nor their husbands know what it is or what it leads to. They are Bolsheviks and don't know it. So are most of those 100 historians that Wilson took abroad with him in the foolish idea that history can teach you the proper demarcations of races, nations and peoples geographically."

There is nothing in the civilized world by which to measure the overturn in Russia.

Charles R. Crane of Chicago, New York and Constantinople, world-around traveler and probably the best informed American on Russia tells me: "Russia is gone and it will be many years before it comes back; it is the foreign element and not the Russian that is now dominant through Bolshevism, the holding of hostages and the disarmament or destruction of all who are not in agreement with this foreign element allied most closely with Germany."

Dr. Dillon, foremost European correspondent tells me: "There is nothing by which to measure the overturn in Russia except the Taeping Rebellion.

"In 1850 a Chinese peasant started a fanatical revolution in the interior of China. The government fought and some brigands came to the side of the peasant. Then another tribe of brigands joined them and the thing went on for many years until General Gordon went in there and quelled the insurrection after twenty million people had been killed. This is where he got the name 'Chinese' Gordon."

I asked Charles R. Crane concerning his relation with Lincoln Steffens and how far Washington was responsible for permission to Trotzky to pass from America to Russia against the protests of the English. Crane replied: "I told Steffens I was going to Russia and he said he would like to come along, but he never saw anything of Russia. On the ship and at Petrograd he was always with the East Side Jews,—the 60 revolutionists who crossed in the same ship with us from Halifax. All I knew of Trotzky was that I saw him screaming and scratching as he lay on the deck of the steamer at Halifax fighting against being taken off. Two British soldiers took him up by the legs and arms and dropped him in a boat. Then the radicals bombarded the politicians and the government officials with assistance of Lincoln Steffens, who wrote telegrams for these New York revolutionists making protest around the world. When word came from Russian authorities requesting that Trotzky be sent through, the British permitted his passage. But I am certain that Wilson had nothing to do with Trotzky going to Russia.

"I saw Lincoln Steffens in Petrograd, but I couldn't induce him to go down to Moscow. He never saw anything of Russia or the Russians, only the East Side Jews. He could learn just as much in New York City. Why he should pose as an authority on Russia is past my comprehension.

"The most promising thing about Russia

today is in the 25,000 Czecho-Slovaks who hold Siberia. They are the cleanest troops and the cleanest men in the world.

"No army ever functioned more perfectly. When these Czecho-Slovaks moved into a town they would in two days have control of all the town utilities, have everything organized and if it was the season for it, garden planting would be begun.

"They have a wonderful intelligence bureau and when Trotzky had made them fair promises of safe transit to Vladivostok whence they were to take passage for France, their intelligence system told them the real situation.

"When their train arrived at a railway station there were machine guns drawn up to blow them in pieces. The Czecho-Slovaks had only one rifle to every twenty men, but they rushed the machine gunners and captured the guns. They carried everything before them in Siberia until an armored train came from the west against them. Then they sent a division, for five days without food, on a distant circuit to get back of that train. At a given signal the Czecho-Slovaks in the east started to run away from the armored train. The Bolshevik troops left the train and pur-

A WORLD REMAKING

sued them and then the Czecho-Slovak division that had circled the country came up and captured the armored train.

"Trotzky and the Bolsheviks and the Russian police took their orders from Berlin.

"Germany had a college in East Prussia to teach all the arts of revolution. The Russian and the Jew are exact antipodes. The Russians are a peace-loving people, but the Jews fish in troubled waters. They will buy up Russian art galleries and pictures and take their chance for getting them out of Russia. They will buy a damaged hotel or other property and take their chance as to title.

"All the Russians were put out of office by the Jews who now absolutely control the country. In Russia a workman with a kit of tools is a capitalist and cannot join the Soviet.

"My hotel in Moscow was bombarded while the Y. M. C. A. and Red Cross workers were there. The Bolsheviks said they could make no distinction. They were capitalists and all capitalists must be put down.

"The Russian people do not dare to move against the Jew leaders and Bolsheviks, as hundreds of the best men in Russia will be killed if anything happens to Lenine and

SOCIALISM VERSUS DEMOCRACY

Trotzky, who are living at the Imperial palaces and exercising more authority than any autocrat of Europe or Russia ever dreamed of exercising.

"The Constantinople College, of which I am president, has about 400 women students. It has educated all the women that have been educated in the southeast of Europe and it has functioned perfectly during the war.

"I have recently returned from Japan, and the people who think Japan will dominate China are in error. The Chinese are getting very jealous of the Japanese. They are building railroads well and running them well.

"There were three rice riots in Japan while I was there. Some smart Aleck bought up all the rice and the people rebelled.

"Japan has had as much trouble as anybody else with high prices and the high cost of living.

"The real Russians hate both the Japanese and the Germans."

Dining in London with a personal friend of Kerensky's, I got an interesting sidelight upon that former political leader. He said:

"Kerensky's fault was lack of decision and refusal to use force. He declared the Russian revolution was a political movement and only political movements should be used in counter and that no force should be resorted to. While we were urging him to arrest Lenine and Trotzky we were ourselves arrested by their forces and thrown into jail.

"The withdrawal of one-half million troops from the southern parts of Russia allowed the Bolsheviks to get supplies which gave them lease of life for many months. Nevertheless people are starving in Petrograd. There has been no general division of the land in Russia. It is all declared the property of the state and the peasants are now clamoring for title to the land they cultivate. But, of course, the Soviet government can not give them title, as there must be no private capital either in lands or machinery.

"There was formerly communal land for the peasants, but it was originally provided that this communal land should be returned to the government each twelve years for reallotment.

"The Russian peasants, of course, objected to this. But the Bolshevik government does not improve their situation."

XXII

War's Inventions For Ships.

Homeward Bound.

VERY few passengers are allowed on the bridge of transatlantic liners. That bridge has become expanded in the modern vessel until it is now one vast workshop as well as officers' hotel. It was first expanded to a steering room, then by chartroom, then by captain's quarters; and now it embraces extended officers' quarters and the most important adjunct to a ship, wireless offices with their rooms of machinery and duplicate machinery. The bridge has practically become a deck.

There have been wonderful inventions during the war in wireless work and wireless mechanics and most of them are still held as war secrets.

High land towers for wireless operations are probably a thing of the past. No longer do you note sparks on a mass of wires over

A WORLD REMAKING

the ships. You can now receive wireless messages in a wooden or brick house with the windows closed and no outside connection. The Tesla theory is being adopted that the vibrations go through the earth and not through air.

Berlin can practically talk with the world so far as the world has apparatus to receive, and it requires only a $200 wireless receiver to hear everything around the world on any wave. A wireless operator told me that he was once in Argentina with a wireless receiver concealed in a bed of flowers on the mantel, and he was able to read everything passing around the world. Working stations in England can hear the sending from California stations.

There are three big Marconi stations already set up for world-around service after the war. In March this year the Marconi people were successful in crossing the North Atlantic with wireless telephone, but that department is still in the experimental stage.

It is highly probable that there will never be another ocean cable built; but for some time there will be work enough for all cables. The necessity for international law and international agreement is now greater than ever.

WAR'S INVENTIONS FOR SHIPS

It took many generations to make the law of the sea. Now there must be international law for the atmosphere.

International agreement is being rapidly formulated and under the existing international codes the shore stations regulate the ship work and give ships their turn in sending.

Ocean liners have three wireless operators working in relays of four hours each, but in active wartime the relays run in two hours, as a man cannot be relied upon for more than two hours' steady wireless work.

The danger in wireless operation is that it may become too common. An outfit is not expensive and a wireless machine that can take or send anything up to ten thousand meter waves costs only a few thousand dollars. Some apparatus can go as high as 25,000 meter waves, but the normal working wave on the ocean is one of six hundred meters. The lowest working wave is that used by airplanes and runs between 50 and 100 meters.

If the apparatus is rightly attuned, 600-meter waves will not interfere with 700-meter waves and so on up, making hundreds of new additional zones for wireless telegraphy.

A WORLD REMAKING

What is the sense of additional investments in ocean cables when the atmosphere or earth itself will now permit more than two hundred different beds, wave lengths or electric zones in which wireless operations may be simultaneously conducted!

While during the war the ears and voice of the ship have been so mightily improved, down in the bottom of the ship another pair of ears has been expanded by the submarine signal development, so that movements may be heard indicating approaching ships, submarines or shores.

Has anything been done for the eye of a ship? Certainly; in front of the big chartroom is a big wheelhouse where the steersman knows nothing concerning where the ship is going except as a voice gives him the direction from the bridge and he follows with his eye on the illuminated compass by the wheel. The safety of the ship is with the lookout and as the center of the bridge is now glass encased, it is quite important that a glass front show clear at all times.

Now in rain, sleet or snow or freezing or foggy weather the lookout on the bridge does not open a window or wipe a pane of glass. If he doubts the clearness of his vision he

WAR'S INVENTIONS FOR SHIPS

touches a switch by the window frame and a circle of glass in the center of the window revolves at great speed and ensures him vision, perfectly free and clear.

Later you will probably see the same invention in the glass fronts of touring automobiles.

Abroad, or crossing the ocean one hears many tales of individual heroism and hardship on both land and sea. Only those are worth noting that are record-breakers.

I have heard people boast of their ability to stay up all night and do good work the next day. Some have kept their post in hospital, war or political warfare, for two nights and days without sleep. But, crossing the ocean, I got a record that I think will stand for a long time without parallel. Captain Wolfe, staff captain of the Aquitania, told me at luncheon one day as follows when I asked him if he had ever been torpedoed.

"Yes, I was torpedoed in October, 1917, 500 miles off the west coast of Ireland. There were 89 in the crew and 47 were saved. Two boats capsized and two reached the Irish coast. There were 27 with me in my boat and for five days and nights I had to hold the tiller and ride the waves with only a few feet of sail and a gale behind.

"I never before thought people could go five days and nights without sleep, but nobody would take the helm from me and I had to steer that boat straight through every wave crest. Of course, we were all drenched through and through. Five days later we were picked up off the Lizard in the English Channel. It took me two months in the hospital to recover my nerve and get back into the sleep habit. The hospital was more terrible than the fight for life on the ocean. At first, I would wake up in bed in a dripping perspiration and with such horrible nightmares that it was some time before I dared get back into bed again."

XXIII

INFLATION AND INTERNATIONAL TRADE.

JUNE, IN WALL STREET.

FIVE years ago, in my book on the Federal Reserve Act, I tried to make clear that any government banking system that would remove the panic possibilities from pig and pork, would do the same for stocks and bonds; that if the Nebraska farmer would have, as he ought to have, government assistance to make finance as regular as transportation, the Wall Street man—and Wall Street is the whole country—would have the same banking assistance, defending his markets. In other words, the farmer and the investor, the pork raiser and the value raiser would have protection from the same reservoir of national credit.

The democratic tariff got in its work ahead of the federal reserve act. Foreign importation made idle men and idle machinery in the

States until the war shut off importations and put the greatest possible tariff wall around the country. Then the Federal Reserve Act became the greatest ally of the Allies. The government stabilized prices, and the civilized world, first with American financial assistance and next with American military assistance, downed autocracy threatening a world conquest and world enslavement.

Now for the first time the Federal Reserve Act comes into play in sustaining industry and values.

World-wide confidence has been established in the new American Reserve banking system. The financial powers now see that in the federal reserve act there was more than one hundred billions of possible credit expansion and that a world war used scarcely one-tenth of it.

The problem now is how to make the United States financial system of international benefit, giving sustenance to the people in need with security for those who meet the human wants.

The difficulty is that Germany with the best banking system in the world was before the war reaching for world trade on long credits, while England was sturdily holding her own in the world markets and the United

INFLATION AND INTERNATIONAL TRADE

States was content with intensive home development based on short credits and individual indebtedness.

If foreign people wanted our wheat, pork or cotton, they sent their representatives here and bought it and did the financing at home.

The United States has never been organized through boards of trade, committees, or kartel combinations to seek foreign business.

Today the United States is the reservoir of the uncrippled energies of the world, the surplus food, the surplus gold, surplus credit and the surplus machinery. All that is lacking are ships and organization. The ships are under international regulation and must so remain for some time.

The United States producers are now permitted by law to organize for export trade. But export trade cannot now build upon the basis of American 60 or 90-day credits. There must be at least two to three years' credit extended to prostrate countries.

We cannot ship machinery, tools, clothing, boots and seeds or foundation stock and expect under existing conditions to get our full pay from the first season's harvest.

A WORLD REMAKING

Unless the American business men and their bankers promptly organize for the extension of long American credits, the United States industrial structure can not be maintained on its present basis of high wage prosperity. It is not and should not be a question of trade rivalry or getting advantage of the other fellow. It is wholly a question of doing our individual and national duty in a world reconstruction, and securing for the future our proper part in a world industrial system, promoting the welfare of man by the exchange of commodities, mutually advantageous.

Already advantageous business offered this country has been forced elsewhere because we have not yet the proper international credit organization.

What is wanted is the same spirit in allied government co-operation for peace reconstruction and sound international merchandising that was manifested in war's destruction, and we need the same united investment interests and banking credits.

We can not stop to educate the world to a United States system. We must deal with what the world has to offer and go forward on established international systems.

INFLATION AND INTERNATIONAL TRADE

Meanwhile there is great danger that American energies may be deflected to appreciation of home values.

We are faced with the speculatively attractive situation that labor values are now far beyond property and security values.

The world calls for housebuilding, but the labor building the house demands wages commensurate with a war living cost. This means a housebuilding and industrial construction program on a war wage basis.

With government control removed as respects rents and commodity prices, the value of the old structure must steadily appreciate to the value of new ones.

When there is a great backlog of American credit values can be talked upon the basis of replacement costs. This means the solidification of war values in new construction and primarily the lifting of old values to the same basis.

With money to finance the new construction on a war wage basis, there will inevitably be money and credit to finance the lifting of former property values to nearly the same basis.

Indeed, going concerns are usually worth more than new ones.

A WORLD REMAKING

New York needs one hundred new hotels and from Maine to Texas thousands are needed. Few have been built since Mr. Wilson came into power. Yet the United States has increased in population, wealth, business and travel.

If it costs 50% more than six years ago to build hotels, must not hotel values advance 50% before a new one can be profitably erected?

If a going mill is earning interest upon ten million in bricks, mortar and machinery, can its rival be built for fifteen or twenty millions before the older mill has considerably appreciated in value?

This is the second inflation and may be called the war labor inflation.

As never before the world has summoned gold from the pockets of the people and placed it under banking reserves. The gold production is declining because of the wage inflation, but the gold concentration makes for a new and distinct inflation. It gives confidence to the banker, the depositor and the check user. The gold standard has been tried out in an unimaginable crisis and has stood the test far better than expected.

INFLATION AND INTERNATIONAL TRADE

The panic value and the corner value and the war value have all been taken out of gold. And gold has been put into bank reserve service to a greater extent than was ever dreamed possible.

The lessened production of gold and the world-wide labor inflation, with stability of credit on the gold standard basis, have brought silver forward to its rightful place as a division of gold in labor payments.

What was formerly feared as silver inflation is now welcomed as a relief from gold inflation, and the world can say "sixteen to one" or any other relative valuation any time it pleases with no financial disturbance.

The above are fundamental and somewhat permanent forms of inflations, but the real giant inflation made by the war, and for the most part unobserved, must be treated in the next article.

XXIV

Inflation By Currency, War Bonds and Taxes

June, in Wall Street.

VERY few financial or economic minds seem to have grasped the factors that are now boiling the American share market.

Most people understand that there is inflation by war and labor and currency. These would be unimportant and measurably temporary were they not reinforced by giant factors never before prevailing in the civilized world. Important among these is the federal reserve act as explained in the previous article discussing five forms of inflation now operative in the war readjustment period. Three other forms of inflation must now be presented.

The Civil War made this country familiar with currency and paper forms of inflation. Recently people have been noting the advance during the war of our circulating medium

THE CAUSES OF INFLATION

from below $40 per capita to above $50 per capita and many have attempted to account for the rise in prices by such puerile inflation as the addition of a billion or two in the circulation medium of these expanding United States. It is hardly worth considering, but it must be mentioned. The real paper expansion has taken place abroad.

France has advanced her paper circulation from six billion francs to 36 billion francs. Yet the addition of this 30 billion francs or six billion dollars has not in France made a redundant currency or one calling for inflation except in food prices. And here it is difficult to separate the war demand from any possible currency inflation.

The singular fact about the expansion of French paper is that it has been absorbed largely in the French investment stocking—practically six billion dollars of non-interest bearing war debt.

French economists now declare that the safety of the world and the redemption of the war debt must be by inflation and that the franc can be considered as practically of half its former value.

A WORLD REMAKING

East of the Rhine paper continues to issue to pay a million men in idleness and to bring food from the country into the cities.

In Russia the printing press has endeavored to put civilization, property, wealth and exchange to the sword. But the sword has only pierced the heart of Russia and summoned international socialism to its own funeral.

The relatively small amount of paper issued in England has not caused the English inflation; there it is solely the war demand and the determination of the empire to give improved wages and conditions to labor.

In England, France and the United States the great factor in inflation is the war bond.

In a world that has only ten billion of gold, eighty-five billions of war debt has been placed upon the three leading allied nations.

So far from being regarded as a mortgage indebtedness depreciating equities in the national valuation, it has the practical effect of interest-bearing currency inflating values and valuations.

An individual and a country can be as poor as they feel, but they can likewise be as rich as they feel. It is the sentiment and the

THE CAUSES OF INFLATION

liquid character of wealth and riches that make expenditure, prosperity and inflation.

Let us illustrate by England. Suppose we conservatively value Great Britain at 80 billion dollars before the war. A theoretical economist will tell you that if you put a mortgage or national debt of 40 billions on the country, you must subtract the debt from the assets and the country is worth the remaining half or 40 billion dollars.

I have had it out with economists and financiers on both sides of the water and have declared that as a practical matter you add the debt to the national wealth and do not subtract it. Every man's individual experience will prove it. And the nation is only the aggregate of the individual experiences.

Does any man in the United States consider that his home, his farm or his factory is mortgaged for one-eighth of its value by 25 billions United States war indebtedness?

Does any man in Great Britain stop to reflect that his house or land, castle or estate, is mortgaged 50% with 40 billion dollars of national indebtedness?

On the contrary, every man forgets it except as he pays taxes and grumbles and advances his prices to meet his taxes.

A WORLD REMAKING

Every man in all three countries who has invested in the war loans, and placed them in his box, reckons, not that he has mortgaged his property, but that he has in his strong box interest-bearing securities nearly as good as gold and with which he can liquidate indebtedness or enter any business enterprise. He considers he has there the strongest collateral, holding the broadest market and the fullest borrowing power.

Ask a man with a million dollars in houses, lands or factories to engage in a new enterprise, or speculation, and he will instantly reflect that he cannot afford to mortgage himself for that venture. But if he has one-half million in real estate, factory or other tangible property and one-half million in government funds, he will instantly listen to the proposal and be ready to invest from his strong box of government securities without danger of a foreclosure or impairment of his estate. He reckons his government bonds as additional wealth of the most liquid character. To him, individually, they are interest-bearing currency or bank balances.

The result is 25 billion dollars of new interest-bearing debt in France available for enterprise or speculation; 35 billion in England

THE CAUSES OF INFLATION

and 25 billion in the United States—an average of nearly 30 billion in each country of prime, interest-bearing national indebtedness fundamental for industrial expansion or speculation in recognition of enhancing values made by war's demands, labor advancement and credit inflation based upon increased services of gold and silver and the American federal reserve act.

Nothing approaching such a situation was ever dreamed of in the history of the civilized world. It outranks the invention of the two previous forms of inflation in the history of civilization; first, the invention of banking, and next of the bank-check system.

It is this which has promoted a big cash speculation in France and has given a market for industrial securities in London beyond the ability of the Stock Exchange or the government to control. Before the declaration of the armistice there was a great cash speculation in London in all kinds of industrial securities that were sold over the counter and without record on the Stock Exchange. Rich munition manufacturers from the Midlands brought their gains and their cash to London banks and brokers and invested in rubber, coal, iron, shipping shares, etc. They left the securities with the brokers or bankers and some weeks later they would come to London, look at the quotations, realize their profits and buy something else—all on a cash basis.

Something akin to this is now going on in the United States. There are twelve Wall Streets or banking supports for Wall Street. They are the federal reserve districts. When money is marked up to 6% and 7% in Wall Street the local man may have it in another federal reserve district at 5% and, if in sound local credit, he need not put up his securities. It matters little whether he puts in his industrial shares or bonds, or his Liberty Loan bonds. He can get his money locally and be supported or insured in credit by the Federal Reserve Bank in his district. Instead of paying cash for some industrial security allied with his trade, he need only put up 40% or 50% margin and feel secure.

Panics, Wall Street pinches and margin calls have no longer terrors for him.

There are twenty-two million investors in the United States educated by Uncle Sam to invest in his Liberty Loan bonds—and if need be to borrow.

THE CAUSES OF INFLATION

How can the Washington government, the conservative bankers, or the Federal Reserve System curb any speculation based so largely upon bank cash and so fully reinforced by government bonds?

While these seven forms of inflation are largely operative in the western world of civilization, the United States is promoting an inflation by its drastic taxation laws, regulations and enforcements.

No man of wealth can today afford to sell anything except at a loss. It he holds for a profit, the sharper the advance, the higher the price, the more the government forces him to hold on. Treasury officials say to him in effect: "If you sell now, you give 50 to 80% of your profit to the government. And if you buy later, you may take the later loss yourself."

Therefore how can a man who has Steel common costing him 25 or 50 consider selling the stock at above 100 when he might conclude, a year from now, that it was a good investment at 125?

He might have to pay the government more than one-half of what he received in the sale of his stock and then, if he purchased it later at a higher price and held on during a decline

A WORLD REMAKING

in the next year, he might have to sustain the whole loss and find the government had taken in taxes all that he ever had, or considered he had, in the investment.

Most of the owners of American Woolen common have the stock in their boxes at under $50 per share. Can the men of wealth afford to sell it at a premium over $100? Can they afford any better to sell it at 200 or 250 if they have to pay in taxes more than half of the advance and if labor valuations in factory replacement shows assets above $500?

Take the case of a real estate owner. If he has a property he considers worth $100,000 paying him a fair rental, can he afford to sell it at $150,000 and pay the government the larger part of the $50,000 advance?

If the necessity of a neighboring business compels a purchase, the seller may demand the original price, a fair profit and all that the government will tax him as its share in the profit arising from the transaction.

Thus is inflation promoted in lands, buildings and all forms of property by the ruinous, iniquitious and unjust and uneconomic system of war taxation which Kitchin and his

THE CAUSES OF INFLATION

associates in the South have imposed upon the incomes, business and prosperity of this country—a war taxation far exceeding that existing in any other country outside of the one hundred percent Bolshevik Russia.

XXV

ARE WE TO PAY FOR GERMAN INTRIGUE AT PANAMA?

BOSTON, *August, 1919.*

The world regards Theodore Roosevelt as an embodied personality who added dignity and power to American citizenship and American freedom. He never expected to be remembered by his exploits in Africa and South America; his addresses or his books. But he did declare that his monument was the Panama canal.

Behind the Roosevelt construction of the Panama Canal is a more dramatic story of human force and personality. It was not Theodore Roosevelt who took Panama and made the building of the Canal by the United States a possibility. It was Lieut. Col. Philippe Bunau-Varilla.

William Morton Fullerton, the newspaper correspondent, told me a few weeks ago in Paris that he once asked Roosevelt at Oyster

GERMAN INTRIGUE AT PANAMA

Bay how he could declare that he took the Panama Canal Zone and Roosevelt replied: "I took the Panama Canal Zone, but I took it from Philippe, who handed it to me on a silver platter."

Six months ago I was bound eastward from Halifax on the steamship "Aquitania." Bunau-Varilla on the same steamer was returning to Paris and he fulfilled his promise made previously in the United States that he would some day tell me the inside story of the Panama Revolution.

It took many hours for him to narrate history covering several decades, and the record was only finished at his beautiful home near the Arc de Triomphe in Paris just before I left France.

It is a dramatic story of human personality covering the fight of a generation in foiling the machinations of Germany in its attempt to destroy the spirit of France, prevent the building of the Panama canal, and lay the foundation for an attempted world conquest.

Lieut. Col. Bunau-Varilla was at one time engineer-in-chief for the Panama canal and previously for the French government. It was he who solved the difficulties of the Culebra cut and landslides.

A WORLD REMAKING

In 1869 the Suez canal was opened with the shares at one-half of their par value of $100. There was doubt if the canal would ever be used. Eight years later the shares were $500 each or ten times the price at the opening of the canal.

De Lesseps was never an engineer. He was a diplomat and when French consul in Egypt secured from Mohammed Ali a concession for the construction of the Canal by the French. Had he kept his founders' shares he would have been worth $25,000,000, but he would keep nothing for himself and he let all the profits go to others.

When de Lesseps in 1881 began the flotation of Panama Canal shares, he had become the idol of the French people. They subscribed liberally to the undertaking, and 1,400,000 yards of earth were being moved monthly in 1886-7-8. In 1887 the canal company accepted Bunau-Varilla's idea of a lock canal and in three years the canal could have been opened.

The company offered 720,000,000 francs in bonds for subscription. On the day set for the subscription some mysterious force telegraphed all over France that de Lesseps was dead. There was a panic on the Bourse at

GERMAN INTRIGUE AT PANAMA

the opening and Panama Canal shares fell 100 francs in a day. Therefore only 260,000,000 francs, or less than half the loan, were subscribed. Of course it is now well understood that the German military party engineered that panic.

Instead of the Canal being put into operation, the courts in 1892 condemned de Lesseps and his son to five years' imprisonment for promoting a financial swindle. It had been declared that six million tons would pass through the Canal the first year, and the courts now decreed that the Canal was absolutely impractical.

This wrecking of the Panama Canal enterprise brought distrust of the masses against all the scientific, political, financial and intellectual people of France so that it was impossible for France thereafter to defend herself in war. Bunau-Varilla saw that the corruption which lost the war in 1871, together with the Panama Canal failure, had cut the sinews of the French nation, and endangered the life of his country. He knew that there was then only one power in the world that could make a success of the Panama Canal and thereby restore the confidence of the French people in their leaders. In 1901 he came to the United States to fight the Nicaraguan Canal proposition. He battled alone at first, but finally won out and proved that the Nicaraguan Canal was in a volcanic zone. Twenty days before the final vote was taken St. Pierre Martinique was destroyed by volcanic action.

In July, 1902, the Spooner law was passed whereby Congress authorized the President to build the Nicaraguan Canal if he could not buy the Panama Canal. In the beginning no senator was in favor of Panama. In the end Panama won by 12 votes.

It was in the original concession from Colombia to the French that transfer could not be made to another government without the consent of Colombia. On the passage of the Spooner resolution, the government of Colombia took the initiative and, without being asked, offered to facilitate the transfer of the concession from the French government to the United States.

Two hundred and fifty-five million dollars had been put into the Canal in shares and bonds, of which 50 million had been returned in interest, leaving a net of about 200 million of French money in the Canal. The French sold the Canal concession and its assets to

GERMAN INTRIGUE AT PANAMA

the United States for $40,000,000 and paid a 20% dividend to the individual security holders. It was agreed that the United States should pay $10,000,000 cash to Colombia and $250,000 annual rental.

It was a de facto government in Columbia and a reference to popular vote on such a matter had never been thought of. There was no precedent for it.

Suddenly the papers of Bogota, the capitol of Colombia, burst forth with the demand for a popular vote. Then the agitation against the United States began. The success of the Suez canal was pointed to and it was whispered that Berlin stood ready to lend Colombia the money to build the Panama canal and let the profits of the enterprise go to Colombia. The result was a vote in repudiation of the contract with the United States.

Later the people of Panama, who are cut off from Colombia by a savage forest, rebelled and set up as an independent government. Bunau-Varilla from Paris assisted in this rebellion. He borrowed in Paris the first $100,000. He wrote the declaration of independence for Panama, designed its flag, wrote its constitution copied after that of Cuba, made the plan of campaign, assisted to

A WORLD REMAKING

organize the government and became the representative of the Republic of Panama at Washington and was recognized by all the leading governments of the world.

It was a bloodless revolution; a battle of wits. The Germans had told the Colombians that the United States would go into Nicaragua and fail. Then the Germans would put their money behind Panama and the Colombians would get the profit.

Hay drew up the treaty with Panama. Bunau-Varilla drew a new one giving clearer and simpler terms and the latter was accepted by Hay exactly as written.

Last year Gen. ——— in Paris told Lieut. Col. Bunau-Varilla that the two principal papers in Bogota were still owned by the Germans.

Roosevelt declared: "I have carved my name in Panama." When the Germans came into the open in their fight for the destruction of France, and the conquest of the world, Roosevelt and his sons offered themselves to the cause of American freedom and democracy. Father and one son are dead and a republican Senate now proposes to defame his record and the record of the Republican Party by payment of $25,000,000 to

GERMAN INTRIGUE AT PANAMA

Colombia, for her part in a German conspiracy against the peace of the world.

Colombia parted with whatever rights she had in Panama 40 years ago and her agreement to accept $10,000,000 for her assent to the transfer from the people of France to the people of the United States was assumed by the new Republic of Panama. The people of Panama alone had the natural territorial right to the Panama Canal route. To pay now $25,000,000 to Colombia is an infamous insult to the men living and dead who defeated the Hun at Panama and made possible the uniting of the world's naval force in its defensive warfare against conquest and tyranny.

How is the name of Theodore Roosevelt to stand "carved in Panama?"

If we are to pay $25,000,000 either because German bankers in Colombia and the international exchange market need the money, or to show our good-will toward all South American countries with whom we are more or less in alliance under the Monroe Doctrine, or to establish a precedent in international justice as respects the territorial integrity of nations, the situation should be clearly understood,

A WORLD REMAKING

If we pay Colombia $25,000,000 because we so quickly recognized the new Republic of Panama, may we not by the same rule hereafter be called upon to pay billions to China?

President Wilson is doing exactly the same thing to China that President Roosevelt did to Colombia—and worse. President Wilson recognizes the right of Japan to take at Shantung 38,000,000 of the best population of China and a rich territory as large as the five New England states outside of Vermont. If the United States Senate approves, why may not the Orient later call upon us for billions of indemnity—as the price for peace in the East with both China and Japan; China to recognize Japan's separation of the Shantung Peninsula and Uncle Sam to pay the bill and make everyone happy all around—except the taxpayer in America.

XXVI.

Foundations In International Socialism.

Boston, *October, 1919.*

WHEN somebody asked Jack Johnson if his physical success in the prize ring might indicate the superiority of 'the colored race he quickly replied:

"The orang-outan is far stronger than any human being. Would his physical success indicate the superiority of the orang-outan over man?"

Lenine and Trotzky and their Bolshevik associates in Russia, international socialism and I. W. W.ism, as the outgrowth of Marxian Socialism, all award the palm, the prize and the wage to the orang-outan.

The above words were written in Paris six months ago as the beginning of an article on Bolshevism. But the blot made upon the map of the world by the chaos in Russia is so apparent as to raise doubts as to the value of any further discussion as to what is Bolshevism in Russia. The world is more interested now in the spread of this disease which had its origin in Germany, and was then invited back by the German military authorities to effect the destruction of Russia.

Out of the divided revolutionary forces of Russia, the social democratic party was organized in 1898. This was split in 1903 into two parties known as Mensheviki (minority) led by George Plechhanov a Russian nobleman, scholar and writer, the Bolsheviki (majority) led by Nicolas Lenine of good birth and an author who had suffered in Siberian prisons. Russian autocracy triumphed in 1905 because Lenine and his Bolsheviki party refused support to the Duma and would not work with Plechhanov who opposed autocracy and supported democracy.

When the Constitutionalists triumphed in 1917, Trotzky turned up in Russia and joining Lenine set up the cry of "peace, bread and land." The war's human sacrifice in Russia had been greater than in any other nation and the hunger for land in a country where 93% of the people had nothing was very great.

INTERNATIONAL SOCIALISM

I have spent some time investigating the American responsibility for Trotzky and believe the subject is one well worthy of a thorough airing at Washington. Our secret service records show that Trotzky was formerly known as Braunstein and was for years in the German secret service in Russia. He was ostentatiously expelled from Berlin in August, 1914, but he was not permitted to remain in Paris. When the allies protested his residence in Spain he settled among the East Side Jews in New York City. His connections with Germany and with social revolutionists became known to the officials in Washington and he was under continuous surveillance by secret service men. When the United States was severing relations with Germany, he started a campaign against militarism and for doing away with the United States government. On March 26, 1917, with Emma Goldman on the platform, Trotzky addressed a German meeting in New York. Washington soon had in its record every word said and all the persons present. He declared that he and his associates "were going to Russia to push the revolution as it ought to be pushed. You who stay here must work hand in hand with the revolution in

A WORLD REMAKING

Russia for only in that way can you accomplish revolution in the United States."

When Charles R. Crane of Chicago and Lincoln Steffens arrived at Halifax on April 3 they saw Trotzky on the steamer deck, screeching and scratching. Some British marines picked him up by his hands and heels, dropped him in a boat and with four companions he was lodged in the detention camp at Amherst.

There were on board about 60 East Side Jews and immediately Steffens joined with them in protests to Washington and elsewhere. Lincoln Steffens was later recognized by the police in San Diego, California, as an enemy of the United States and its government and was refused permission to make any public address.

Now the British secret service as well as the American secret service had the full record of Trotzky as a German spy and a promoter of revolutions. It is said that President Wilson had nothing to do with the subsequent release of Trotzky at Halifax, but it is also said that Mr. Wilson had turned over to Louis D. Brandeis the direction of American affairs in connection with Russia. Reports are also conflicting as to a forged

INTERNATIONAL SOCIALISM

telegram from Kerensky requesting passage for Trotzky. But whatever may be eventually revealed as to the sinister influences at work, the release of Trotzky astounded the secret service of both Great Britain and the United States.

Defeat of Democracy.

In London I heard allegations close to high sources that Kerensky has taken money from both Germany and the allies, although his friends stoutly deny the charges. But the "peace, bread and land" cry of Lenine and Trotzky in its destructive influence on Russia was seconded most forcefully by the Kerensky order making the soldiers equal with their officers and forbidding all distinctions in rank. This order has been denounced as a forgery, but it did its work in leveling down all authority. It broke the entire military front of Russia. In November, 1917, the military forces at Moscow and Petrograd went Bolshevik and Kerensky fled.

It was charged against Kerensky that he had not given the promised Constitutionalist assembly with elections based on universal, secret, direct and equal suffrage. But Kerensky had set up the machinery. When the

A WORLD REMAKING

Bolsheviki came into power and counted the votes, they were found to be two to one against Lenine and Trotzky, who thereupon suppressed the Assembly with bayonets after a single day's session. Thus was a dictatorship more oligarchic than that of the Czar given the Russian people in place of the democracy of a representative assembly for which they had been struggling.

The Experiment of Socialism.

Then went into effect the most tragic experiment in Socialism. All the professional and educated classes, all employers, all persons of capital, enterprise or property, all private traders and commercial agents and men of religious orders were excluded from the ballot and disarmed. All teachers, professors, editors, bankers and manufacturers were likewise thrown over the political breastworks and a government was set up as a "Socialistic Federal Republic of Soviets," supported by "a Socialistic Red Army of Workmen and Peasants." All business was taken over by the state and all land declared national property and given without compensation to the laboring people.

INTERNATIONAL SOCIALISM

But any workman in Russia with a kit of tools or who employs a fellow-laborer becomes a capitalist and loses his citizenship.

Whence springs this nightmare blot upon man and his progress in civilization?

The immediate source is German money and German orders. Back of it is the oppression of the Russian people by a government supported by a secret police leagued with and corrupted by Berlin and farther back lie the false teachings of international socialism as expounded by Heinrich Karl Marx, a German Jew born May 15, 1818, at Treves, Rhenish Prussia.

Universal War.

The poison of the lifework of Marx has been spread over the whole world and set labor at war with its best friend, accumulated capital. These Marxian international socialists at times threaten the peace of England and of the United States. They tied up the Swiss transportation system for several days and threatened the government of the oldest republic in the world when the allies were signing the terms of armistice to Germany. They threaten the government of

A WORLD REMAKING

France; but Clemenceau says he hopes to live to see "the vermin" driven off her soil.

The daily press pictures the eruptions of the day. The causes deep down, or the errors of thought in political, economic and social systems, are rarely uncovered at their inception. They must often grow until there is an eruption and threatened corruption of the whole system. For who can say which of the many human vagaries put forth in the world may become potential?

Horace Greeley and the New York *Tribune* could never have dreamed that the guinea a week they paid a fellow by the name of Marx for weekly letters from London was not only the sole support for the Marx family, but the financial foundation for the whole structure of international socialism that later threatened the world. Yet I recently learned in London that such was the fact.

Some time I would like to make broad inquiry as to why so many dangerous men of the world are those who have changed or been changed from the faith into which they were born. The lawyer father of Karl Marx baptised the entire family into Christianity in 1824 when Karl was only six years of age. When he was 23 he was given the degree of

Doctor of Philosophy. In 1843 he studied Socialism at Paris and expounded it in the Rheinische Zeitung, an organ of the most advanced section of the Rheinische radical bourgeoisie and the government that year suppressed it. In that year he also married Jennie von Westphalen, daughter of a high government official and through her mother a lineal descendant of the Duke of Argyle, beheaded under James II.

"Property," said Proudhon, "is the product of society and must be administered as such." With this underlying idea Marx agreed, but declared for the emancipation of society from commercialism and that there was only one class to fight for political emancipation in Germany—the proletariat. In Brussels, Marx and Engels ran a weekly paper and joined the communistic secret society of German workers entitled "The League of the Just." After the German revolution of 1848 Marx and Engels went to Cologne and founded the Neue Rheinische Zeitung with the sub-title "An organ of Democracy." Marx advocated non-payment of taxes and armed resistance. His paper was suspended and he was tried for treason; acquitted, but expelled from Prussia. The

French government would not permit him to reside in Paris and he settled in London where he lived in great financial straits in a room in Dean St., Soho, his sole support being letters to the New York *Tribune* for a guinea a week. His three children died very young; two of them in this home of a single room.

In 1859, Marx published his Critique of Political Economy. This he rewrote in 1867 as "Das Kapital," the present textbook of the socialists throughout the world.

Capital, according to Marx, is the means of appropriating surplus value as distinguished from ground rent. Surplus value is that part of the newly created product which is not given as wage to the workman. The whole philosophy of Marx is founded upon the declaration of Adam Smith that labor produces all things. But the Marx definition of labor would bar out Fulton, McCormick, Bell and Edison, the labor of brain and of enterprise, and the engineering talent always valued at 10% of the structure; and give the world and its direction over to the labor of hand.

Indeed Marx aimed at superseding all existing governments by a vast international

INTERNATIONAL SOCIALISM

combination of workers of all nations without distinction of creed, color, or nationality. A fruitage from Marx's work is to be found in Mr. Wilson's peace pact with Germany which aims to set up a socialistic international labor organization.

The Marx proposal is that land and capital which are requisites of labor and the sources of wealth and culture become the property of society and be managed by it for the general good.

Fourier advocated socialism with a minimum of subsistence to all and the balance 5-12 to labor, 4-12 to capital and 3-12 to talent. It is worthy of note that the Fourier line of socialism of 1-3 to capital and 5-12 to labor has not only been accomplished, but passed as respects the division to labor. In general capital does not get 4-12 or 1-3, and labor gets more than 5-12.

The Marxian theory is not only mind-stifling, but soul-destructive, for man is man from his mind, not from his body. When the animal, the ape, the gorilla, the orang-outan come to the top and attempt to direct the mind of man, mental development must decay.

A WORLD REMAKING

The Marx theory was that capitalism is thievery because it keeps one-third what labor produces. He never recognized that capital was only saved labor, creating machinery or tools for hand labor.

Until Marx arose, the rights of property had never been seriously antagonized except by piracy on the sea and wars, with pillage and conquest on land. The Phoenicians of Tyre and Sidon stood high in world trade for 2000 years because of their honor and probity. Venice held commercial sway for many hundred years because the word of a Venetian merchant was a sacred bond.

But now under Marxian socialism there are to be no bonds and no sacredness—even bonds and sacredness of the family are denied.

In 1864 Marx entered the London International Workingmen's Association and expounded education, trade-unions, working day and co-operation. The Franco-German war, anarchist agitation and the Paris Commune broke up the International Commune, which finally removed to New York in 1872 and dissolved in Philadelphia in 1876.

Marx died in 1882 but his work moves on. It has permeated the whole of Europe and is fighting insidiously through strikes and socialistic organizations for recognition in the United States and the overthrow of American Democracy to be succeeded by the autocracy of those who claim to lead the world's muscle workers.

Marx had the British Museum for his library with its bluebook records of parliamentary investigations into all the bad features of early English industrialism. He had preceding him the work of Robert Owen who aroused England over the condition of her working men and spent 60,000 pounds of his own money to promote his schemes for communism, plans for which he laid before the House of Commons in 1817.

In Owen's time an English worker had no soil, no education and no vote. His wages were low and the rights of combination were denied him until 1824. Improved machinery only drove him into greater poverty. His hours were long and he competed with women and children brought at the ages of five and six from the workhouses.

The picture which Marx painted, supported by blue book investigations, is a terrible picture of English industrialism and unintelligent greedy capitalism.

A WORLD REMAKING

The American revolution, the French revolution, our war of 1812 and the Napoleonic Wars had set the world in a turmoil, and the way to light and liberty had not then been blazoned by the success of the democracy of America. The free individual struggle for wealth and social advantages is comparatively recent.

What Marx proposed,—the whole world in one industrial communistic union,—can be attained only by the path that Germany proposed to world conquest; and then by the overthrow of the autocratic and military dictators. These removed, there would come again the disintegration into nations and states and smaller fighting units.

By the military path attempted in Russia —the sacrifice of all the people at the top, and the setting up of the strongest autocracy at the bottom—the experiment is scarcely on the map before the hands of starvation, disease and death are over all the cities and only people on the land can have existence.

The great blessing to the world may yet be the Russian experiment in Marxian socialism—a picture of horror frightening the whole world—an experiment destroying a nation, but possibly saving western civilization now moving forward under democracy.

In the French revolution and the destruction of the Bastile, only 10,000 were slain.

The experiment in Marxian socialism has reckoned its monthly deathroll in the cities of Petrograd and Moscow alone by the hundred thousand.

Socialism is the poison of democracy and destroys the individual opportunity and—initiative individualism created by democracy.

XXVII.

BOLSHEVIK DANGER AND THE REMEDY.

BOSTON, *October, 1919.*

THE Marxian poison of international socialism has been introduced into the United States by underpaid professors in our leading universities. These men have never yet been able to understand the value in human development of concentrated wealth which gives 90% of its income to the public in useful works, accompanied by experience, engineering talent and economical management as well as initiative in enterprise.

The poison has been spread by the enemies of representative government seeking fruits from disorder—those who fish in troubled waters—by so-called labor organizations and their demagogic agitators and by would-be social reformers who believe that divine justice and true Christianity require the taking from the minority for the temporary blessing

THE DANGER OF BOLSHEVISM

of the majority, little realizing the economic waste for all that must follow.

Its attacks upon business are supported by politicians seeking votes by denunciations of the possessing few, as the robbers of the people and of the hand producers.

In the political agitation that has gone on through two republican and two democratic administrations at Washington, it seems almost to have been forgotten that great as is the Constitution of the United States, its greatness consists in the freedom it secures to individual enterprise and for combinations of enterprise and capital; the protection it gives to individual inventors, and the stimulus it furnishes to individual initiative.

U. S. spells not only "combination" but the dollar mark as the reward for business enterprise which enlarges output, with improving quality and reducing cost.

It is thus that here the people are better and more abundantly fed and clothed; and let it never be forgotten that labor consumes more than 90% of what it produces.

The first answer business naturally makes to demand for increased wages is a compromise by which wages are first increased

A WORLD REMAKING

with a tacit agreement that output shall be improved, bringing in larger revenue. This failing, prices in that line of goods are naturally advanced and labor combinations are encouraged by capital that the prices of the product may be universally raised. Of course the first raisers get the primary advantage, but when advanced wages and restricted hours and output reach the basis of the food supply, wage earners who received the first advance find their advantage not only lost in the higher cost of food, clothing and shelter, but oftentimes more than lost in the balancing of accounts.

Goods, like sugar that were once sold at retail without profit as store advertisement, get out of hand and take on normal profits.

The doubling of wages by international or social warfare more than doubles retail prices because prices and profits must not only be doubled but insurance rates many times increased; and insurance begins to take on many new forms. Producer, jobber and retailer must all be insured and at high rates against a fall in prices with overproduction. Luxury multiplies and demands more service. The cost of distributing

THE DANGER OF BOLSHEVISM

goods, as any department store can testify, has risen from below 10% to about 30%.

The agitation for increased wages to meet the higher prices becomes accentuated and the employer often yields all his profits to maintain his business, hoping for a return to the former or normal basis. At this point the employees in combination may demand not only increased wages at the expense of the capital, but the control of the business.

The most notable examples I found in England. The wage of the railroad people had been more than doubled by the war. Yet they complained that they were worse off by war prices in the cost of living. The net revenue of the railroads was used to pay the wages and the national treasury, taxing all the people, paid the interest and dividends. To raise railroad rates was to still further increase the cost of living. The result I found before I left England was the drilling of troops under secret orders and the quiet marshalling of the military forces to preserve not only order but transportation when strikes and rioting should begin.

The English coal miners complained they could not live on the doubled wages and they demanded the nationalization of the mines with guaranties to cover the cost of living. When asked about improving the deficient output and reducing the costs to the consumer they replied: "We know our own drones and we can throw out of the hive the idle and the useless if we get all the profit," thus threatening another social war within their own borders in the upset of the labor union dogma that the inefficient must be paid the wages of the efficient.

In the States politicians and the government have yielded to the railroad unions, threatening disruption of transportation, until there are no wages left for capital and the demand for higher railroad wages is accompanied by a proposal to surrender the railroads, as having little present value, to the freight brakemen, the engine drivers and their organized co-laborers—with increased lien upon the government treasury.

Now if the railroads do not belong to the owners or to the national treasury that supports them, they belong to the users rather than to the employees who already take the entire net earnings and are demanding the right to eat up the whole.

THE DANGER OF BOLSHEVISM

When capital offers profit-sharing or partnership it is rejected with scorn because there are no assured profits. Capital has now reached the point in the United States where it quite naturally asks for a solution of the labor problem.

There can be no solution except by clear thinking; getting down to fundamental principles as respects wages and profits, capital and labor—the labor of hand as compared with the labor of brain, in initiative, invention and enterprise and as compared with the labor of capital and the horsepower of machinery. For capital is only saved labor insuring enlarged horsepower for the future.

First and foremost has got to be fought out the problem as to whether the Constitution of the United States, protecting the right of the individual to make material progress, to accumulate and to save, is to be protected.

The first reform necessary is to put behind the flag at every schoolhouse the Constitution of the United States. There should never be a graduation certificate or a diploma issued to a West Point cadet, a State university student, a high school scholar or a grammar school pupil who has not passed

A WORLD REMAKING

an examination and shown his knowledge of the meaning of the Constitution of the United States and its representative form of government.

Then when people are asked by politicians high or low to throw their caps in the political ring for a speedy merger of the United States into a superstate directing the economic, naval and military forces of the world, they will be able to inquire as to a supreme court defending the rights of the weak against the strong; and whether taxes are to be levied in justice or under political expediency.

Next after political economics, we must teach social economics through the press, the university, the pulpit and the common school. In the effort to defend itself from destruction, capital has welcomed every sort of proposal whether in the nature of profit-sharing or nationalization without any clear conception of the rights of property, or boundaries as respects wages.

Most profit-sharing schemes have failed because the wage-earner who accepted a given profit regarded it as wages wrongfully withheld. The giving from profits neither stimulated enterprise, initiative, or invention, nor in any way worked for future profits. Both the giver and taker labored under delusions.

Profits Are Not Wages.

The world must be educated to see that profits are not wages and do not belong in the plane of wages, and wages are not profits and do not belong in the plane of profits.

An honest day's work and an honest day's wage is the standard and the law, high and low.

Wages come to the hand of man. Profits come to the brain of man. Between the brain and the hand there must be nerve cords sympathetic with both. Bruise the hand and the brain feels the pain. Bruise the brain and the hand is paralyzed.

The nerve connection between labor of brain and labor of hand is human fellowship.

This could not come into the present new world age until human slavery, making human beings the fellow or the ox, had been abolished. Every empire whether of Southern Cotton, or of Greece or Rome, founded upon human slavery, has gone down.

A WORLD REMAKING

Now brain work and hand work must be recognized as co-laborers. It is the business of the brain to protect the labor of hand. Hence we have success in welfare work and its recognition by contented labor. We have factory sanitation, rest rooms and hospitals, night schools and manual training schools, lectures, moving pictures for instruction and recreation; and protection to the savings of employees. Welfare work has been carried to the home, the milk bottle and the bathroom. It will be gradually extended into cooperative purchases and unions of employees for personal improvement and advancement and to combinations of savings to be put into the business and share in the profits of the business on the true basis of property and accumulated savings.

Not in profit-sharing, but in happiness sharing, will be found the solution as betwixt capital and labor.

As it is the duty of the brain to guard the hand, so it is the duty of every employer and every brain head, whether in management, superintendence or foremanship, to guard and protect the happiness and safety, the continued employment, the savings and the bodily and pocket prosperity of the laborer; with the door opened, through his savings, to enter safely into the field of property, of enterprise, and of profits from savings and thought.

When, instead of the public hospitals, the home nursing for the faithful servant becomes the rule; when the kitchen is furnished with literature and its mental pabulum, and the way for its economic, social and religious instruction, there will be a restoration of the true family relation and the true family happiness. On the same family line is the true factory relation with factory happiness.

XXVIII.

The Principles Under Wages and Profits.

Boston, *October, 1919.*

THE readjustment of the labor situation will not come by the destruction of capital or the expropriation of the fortunes of capitalists. It will come by education, with enough suffering to make these truths universally recognized:

First, that labor must advance itself by joining work of brain with labor of hand.

Second, that there are wages for labor and rewards for thought and not rewards for labor and wages for thought.

Third, as labor consumes 95% of what it produces, restricted production enhancing prices is suicide. The food of the world can not be raised by present eight hour day labor without taking workers from other lines of industry supplying human wants.

WAGES AND PROFITS

Fourth, that capital is the best friend of labor and capital accumulation the only friend for labor of the future, insuring its employment and production.

Fifth, when wages are suddenly doubled as in time of war, the fruitage may be soon found in costs of living more than doubled because there is disorganization and sharp advance in insurance rates.

Sixth, the consumer has no partnership with capital save as a customer demanding honest goods and public safety. To that labor of the living and in that labor of the dead represented by capital, he has no proprietary right.

Seventh, the true partnership of capital, labor and consumer is in an honest understanding by each of the function of the other; that capital is only labor saved and, as capital, works at lower wages and for the benefit of labor, increasing labors wages and multiplying its efforts. Without accumulated capital in the form of machinery, hand labor would live here as formerly, by the fish of the stream and the game of the forest, and there would have to be starvation and reduction of population to the limits of the food of forest and stream.

A WORLD REMAKING

The subject may be still further illuminated by the annexed correspondence:

BOSTON, *August, 1919.*

To the editor of the Boston News Bureau:

The greatest question before civilization today is the readjustment of the labor situation.

The present system of hiring labor is but a derivation from the system of buying it which prevailed 2000 years ago in Roman days. Your page and many other articles indicate the widespread and deep conviction that the old order is changing and that some new system must be evolved. What shall the new order be? We may start with the axiom that both capital and labor are essential in any industrial enterprise. The question is, what are their just relative emoluments and rewards? It has been assumed in the past and has become ingrained in our consciousness that management of the enterprise and the resulting net profits belong by rights to the owner, but the future will show us that this conception is as vicious as that the bodily ownership of one human being by another in past ages was.

WAGES AND PROFITS

The day is dawning when it will be perceived that partnership between all the interests involved, namely, capital, labor and consumers must prevail.

J. P. S.

THE ANSWER.

IN MICHIGAN,
September, 1919.

J. P. S.—

Your statements are rather sweeping. If they are just, you and I and our grandchildren will not live long enough to see the new world or the Heaven which you describe.

The world is made up of good and bad —a lot of bad in the best of us and a lot of good in the worst of us,—and you cannot have equal division of the fruitage of civilization, enterprise or industry until you have equality in the integrity of each individual: the aim to do the best he can with the human machine, the mind and body which the Creator has given him. Make equal division of the fruit and you lessen the incentive to production, not only universally, but individually. The evil will not work to their full capacity and the good will refuse to

A WORLD REMAKING

work under the injustice which puts the major effort upon them without the major reward.

There is no difference between hiring labor and buying labor. Formerly to get the labor you bought the man and you had to provide for him, clothe him, feed him and lodge him, and it was the most expensive form of labor in the world. The damage to the world was not that the slave remained a slave, but that the free man became a brute, and labor which alone redeems and regenerates man was degraded. Every structure, social, economic and national, that rested on slave labor, fell to pieces.

The slave man was not recognized as brother, only as an ox to be fed and worked. Man in the progress of civilization is no longer brother to the ox. He is fellow worker with his employer, whether on farm or in factory, on his own terms or in combination with others. His right in his product does not extend beyond his wage payment. If he completes or mends for you a shoe, he has no claim on your foot. If he delivers a barrel of pork, a gallon of milk, a pound of butter, a bushel of potatoes, or a

THE ANSWER

tailor-made suit, to you for money, or for wages, he has no claim upon the consumer.

Any merging of wages and profits for a general redistribution of the same is communism and the destruction of individual initiative, individual invention and individual incentive to improve the product, enlarge the output and reduce the cost.

By these three incentives and these three results is the progress of civilization so far as it relates to man's physical efforts in respect to food, fuel, clothing and shelter.

Maintain this individual initiative; maintain the incentive to labor, to invent and to improve, by giving the inventor and the improver due rewards for his invention and improvement—continue the incentive to save and accumulate with the right to transmit property in safety to the family—and you continue the world's material and spiritual progress.

You continue the world's spiritual progress as you continue to define and make clear the relations of man to his fellow man. You continue the world's material progress as you convert labor into capital and preserve the capital as machinery for the employment of more labor.

A WORLD REMAKING

Both the spiritual and material development of man require the uprooting of the two fallacies that labor is punishment for sin and that happiness is associated with wealth.

When man comes to know his brother and to labor for his brother in the true spirit of human service, he will see both work and labor, —of brain and hand—God's greatest gifts to man and the only source of happiness; and that there can be no true happiness associated with wealth where wealth is not so administered as to promote the common good.

The true employer today is the fellow laborer, and if he does not elevate the labor associated with him he is the great loser. The world lost when labor was a slave. The world produced its finest when the workman worked in his home with his apprentice by his side. That farm produced the most happiness where the hired man was a part of the family circle and worthy of it.

Now bonds of slavery and serfdom have been sundered for man's progress in a new era of light and truth and happiness. In the future all men will be found what, in reality, they now are, fellow-laborers and each will recognize what he does not now,

THE ANSWER

that every man is different from every other man, makes a different product and both here and hereafter receives a different reward.

The Creator never made two human being just alike, never decreed that humanity should dwell under one tree, or in one kind of house, or think, or act or produce except in infinite variety.

That individuality, that individual variety, must be protected for the finest fruitage of humanity; and the greatest economic protection is in protection of the awards which must be individualized and not communized.

Very truly yours,

CLARENCE W. BARRON.

THE END.

Trieste Publishing has a massive catalogue of classic book titles. Our aim is to provide readers with the highest quality reproductions of fiction and non-fiction literature that has stood the test of time. The many thousands of books in our collection have been sourced from libraries and private collections around the world.

The titles that Trieste Publishing has chosen to be part of the collection have been scanned to simulate the original. Our readers see the books the same way that their first readers did decades or a hundred or more years ago. Books from that period are often spoiled by imperfections that did not exist in the original. Imperfections could be in the form of blurred text, photographs, or missing pages. It is highly unlikely that this would occur with one of our books. Our extensive quality control ensures that the readers of Trieste Publishing's books will be delighted with their purchase. Our staff has thoroughly reviewed every page of all the books in the collection, repairing, or if necessary, rejecting titles that are not of the highest quality. This process ensures that the reader of one of Trieste Publishing's titles receives a volume that faithfully reproduces the original, and to the maximum degree possible, gives them the experience of owning the original work.

We pride ourselves on not only creating a pathway to an extensive reservoir of books of the finest quality, but also providing value to every one of our readers. Generally, Trieste books are purchased singly - on demand, however they may also be purchased in bulk. Readers interested in bulk purchases are invited to contact us directly to enquire about our tailored bulk rates. Email: customerservice@triestepublishing.com

You May Also Like

New Zealand. Decisions of the Speakers of the House of Representatives on Points of Order, Rules of Debate and General Practice of the House, 1867 to 1888, Inclusive

C. C. N. Barron

ISBN: 9780649560387
Paperback: 154 pages
Dimensions: 5.0 x 0.33 x 8.0 inches
Language: eng

The Swedish Revolution Under Gustavus Vasa

Paul Barron Watson

ISBN: 9780649716753
Paperback: 328 pages
Dimensions: 6.14 x 0.69 x 9.21 inches
Language: eng

www.triestepublishing.com

You May Also Like

Elements of Logic: On the Basis of Lectures; With Large Supplementary Additions

William Barron & James R. Boyd

ISBN: 9780649571932
Paperback: 266 pages
Dimensions: 6.14 x 0.56 x 9.21 inches
Language: eng

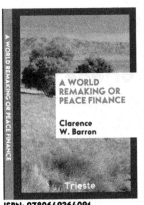

A world remaking or peace finance

Clarence W. Barron

ISBN: 9780649364091
Paperback: 268 pages
Dimensions: 6.14 x 0.56 x 9.21 inches
Language: eng

www.triestepublishing.com

You May Also Like

Report of the Department of Farms and Markets, pp. 5-71

Various

ISBN: 9780649333158
Paperback: 84 pages
Dimensions: 6.14 x 0.17 x 9.21 inches
Language: eng

Catalogue of the Episcopal Theological School in Cambridge Massachusetts, 1891-1892

Various

ISBN: 9780649324132
Paperback: 78 pages
Dimensions: 6.14 x 0.16 x 9.21 inches
Language: eng

www.triestepublishing.com

You May Also Like

Three Hundred Tested Recipes

Various

ISBN: 9780649352142
Paperback: 88 pages
Dimensions: 6.14 x 0.18 x 9.21 inches
Language: eng

A Basket of Fragments

Anonymous

ISBN: 9780649419418
Paperback: 108 pages
Dimensions: 6.14 x 0.22 x 9.21 inches
Language: eng

Find more of our titles on our website. We have a selection of thousands of titles that will interest you. Please visit

www.triestepublishing.com

You May Also Like

Three Hundred Tested Recipes

Various

ISBN: 9780645352143
Paperback, 92 pages
Dimensions: 6.14 x 0.16 x 9.21 inches
Language: eng

A Basket of Fragments

Anonymous

ISBN: 9781374886-5679
Paperback, 108 pages
Dimensions: 6.14 x 0.18 x 9.21 inches
Language: eng

Find more of our titles on our website. We have a selection of thousands of titles that will interest you. Please visit

www.fireatepublishing.com

Lightning Source UK Ltd.
Milton Keynes UK
UKOW06f1512231017

311488UK00007B/1856/P